Agropolitics in the
European Community

William F. Averyt, Jr.

The Praeger Special Studies program—
utilizing the most modern and efficient book
production techniques and a selective
worldwide distribution network—makes
available to the academic, government, and
business communities significant, timely
research in U.S. and international economic, social, and political development.

Agropolitics in the European Community

Interest Groups and the
Common Agricultural Policy

PRAEGER SPECIAL STUDIES IN INTERNATIONAL POLITICS AND GOVERNMENT

Praeger Publishers   New York   London

Library of Congress Cataloging in Publication Data

Averyt, William F   1944-
    Agropolitics in the European Community.

    (Praeger special studies in international politics
and government)
    Bibliography: p.
    Includes index.
    1. Agriculture and state—European Economic Community
countries.   2. Pressure groups—European Economic
Community countries.   I. Title.
HD1920.5.Z8   1977   338.1'84   77-10619
ISBN 0-03-039666-2

PRAEGER SPECIAL STUDIES
200 Park Avenue, New York, N.Y., 10017, U.S.A.

Published in the United States of America in 1977
by Praeger Publishers,
A Division of Holt, Rinehart and Winston, CBS, Inc.

789   038   987654321

Printed in the United States of America

This study was written under grants from the Carnegie Endowment for International Peace and from the Social Science Research Council. The assistance of these organizations is gratefully acknowledged; they are not responsible for any of the views expressed herein. I must also thank the Council of European Studies and the Deutscher Akademischer Austauschdienst for a grant to study German at the Technische Universitat in Berlin.

The officials of the Commission of the European Communities, the German Ministry for Food, Agriculture, and Forests, the French Ministry of Agriculture and Rural Development, the Deutscher Bauernverband, the Fédération Nationale des Syndicats d'Exploitants Agricoles, the Association Générale des Producteurs de Blé, and the Comité des Organisations Professionnelles Agricoles (COPA) were most helpful in granting me interviews and furnishing documents. I am especially indebted to M. André Herlitska, secretary-general of COPA, and to his staff for the exceptional cooperation they extended to me.

The resources of the following libraries were indispensable: Université Libre de Bruxelles; Fondation Nationale des Sciences Politiques, Paris; Bibliothèque Royale, Brussels; and the library of the Commission of the European Communities.

The ideas that formed the basis for my book appeared first in my article "Eurogroups, Clientela, and the European Community" in volume 29, number 4 of *International Organization*, published by the Regents of the University of Wisconsin.

Madame K. Lakdar of the Information Office of the Commission greatly assisted me with interviews and research materials. I profited from the conferences on the European Communities sponsored by the Carnegie Endowment and held at Columbia University, the City University of New York, and Cornell University in 1974 and 1975.

I am deeply indebted to Joseph LaPalombara, who provided valuable direction for this study, as well as to James Fesler and H. Bradford Westerfield for their insightful comments.

Finally, my thanks to Anne for her research support and moral encouragement during our gypsy life of the past few years and to my twins, Alan and Kevin, without whose arrival I would have written this much sooner.

CONTENTS

LIST OF TABLE AND FIGURES

LIST OF ABBREVIATIONS

AGPB	Association Générale des Producteurs de Blé
CAP	Common agricultural policy
CNIEL	Centre National Interprofessionnel de l'Economie Laitière
CNJA	Centre National des Jeunes Agriculteurs
COMEPRA	Comité Européen pour le Progrès Agricole
COPA	Comité des Organisations Professionnelles Agricoles
DBLN	Deutscher Bundesverband der Landwirte im Nebenberuf
DBV	Deutscher Bauernverband
EC	European Community
ECSC	European Coal and Steel Community
EEC	European Economic Community
EVSt	Einfuhr- und Vorratstellen
FEOGA	Fonds Européen d'Orientation et de Garantie Agricole
FFA	Fédération Française de L'Agriculture
FNB	Fédération Nationale Bovine
FNPL	Fédération Nationale des Producteurs de Lait
FNSEA	Fédération Nationale des Syndicats d'Exploitants Agricoles
FORMA	Fonds d'Organisation et de Régularisation des Marchés Agricoles
GEA	Groupement National pour la Défense et le Développement des Enterprises Agricoles
MODEF	Mouvement de Défense des Exploitants Familiaux
MONATAR	Mouvement National des Travailleurs Agricoles et Rurales
ONIBEV	Office National Interprofessionnel du Bétail et de la Viande
ONIC	Office National Interprofessionnel des Céréales
UA	unit of account

Agropolitics in the European Community

1

EUROPEAN FARMERS AND THE COMMON AGRICULTURAL POLICY

In recent years the common agricultural policy has seemed the only solid accomplishment holding the European Community (EC) together. In the 1970s, when rising oil prices caused fertilizer costs to soar, when poor weather and world population growth placed huge demands on world food supplies, when a superpower such as the United States announced it would use food as a political weapon, the Community's common agricultural policy received renewed attention from political leaders in Europe and throughout the world.

The common agricultural policy resulted from a set of complex compromises among European interests, and it thus provides a good illustration of EC politics. The final decisions of the Council of Ministers in Brussels result from the resolution of national, regional, producer, and consumer interests.

Community farmers quickly organized to make their voices heard in EC institutions. They had little choice. By the mid-1960s, decisions on farm prices and protection against foreign competition had shifted from Paris and Bonn to Brussels. No longer could the Saxon wheat farmer or the milk producer in Hainaut affect these decisions merely by using his national farmers' association to lobby the national parliament or the ministry of agriculture. New centers of decision, such as the European Commission, now drafted proposals on the following year's wheat prices, and other bodies such as the Council of Ministers made the final decisions on these proposals.

Another factor that impelled European farmers to organize a new kind of interest group across national boundaries was the common agricultural policy itself. It was the first and remains the most massive example of interventionist community policy in the economic sphere. It requires constant monitoring and administration; its effects are immediately visible in the form of higher or lower farm incomes and cheaper or more expensive butter in grocery stores from Palermo to Hamburg. This accounts for the fact that the common agricultural policy, alone among EC policies, has made prolonged contact with Europeans at the grass-roots level: It touches fundamental concerns of all citizens of the member states, be they farmers or consumers.

The salience of the agricultural policy is demonstrated by its claim on Community resources. In the mid-1960s, it occupied 70 percent of the ministers' time in the Council and used up 95 percent of the EC budget.[1]

Once the EC had rearranged the national patterns of decision making in the agricultural field, how precisely did EC farmers alter their political strategies? How did national farm organizations pursue their goals in a political arena that was no longer purely national? Did the new EC system offer new and better opportunities for farm leaders to influence policy? Did it present new kinds of obstacles?

In order to do justice to the complexity of EC farm politics, this study focusses on the national farm groups of two EC states, France and the Federal Republic of Germany. It then examines farm politics in each nation before and after the formation of the common agricultural policy. This provides a perspective on the changes with which national farm organizations had to cope in the early 1960s. The new Community-level farmers' group, the Comité des Organisations Professionnelles Agricoles (COPA), is then analyzed. COPA provides a good example of a supranational or (perhaps more accurately) a transnational interest group. It is certainly one of the strongest and oldest of the Community-level groups, which will be referred to as Eurogroups in order to distinguish them from national interest groups.

Finally, the different kinds of strategies now available to Community farm leaders are examined. Because the EC institutions represent another level of government superimposed on the older national systems, the potential political strategies available to interest-group leaders have become considerably more complex.

A word should be said about the choice of France and Germany as the two member states to be studied. The story of the EC may be seen, somewhat simplistically, as the compromise between German industry and French agriculture. In a broader framework, the Community represents one aspect of the evolving Franco-German relationship, and the EC began with an explicit agreement between Charles de Gaulle and Konrad Adenauer on this subject.[2]

France and Germany provide an interesting contrast in the area of farm politics. France had much to gain from the common agricultural policy and promoted it strongly in Brussels. Germany's main concerns were commercial and industrial instead of agricultural. Yet the one-eighth of the German work force that was in agriculture in 1961 voted mainly for the Christian Democrats, whose dominance of German politics did not end until 1969. Bonn therefore could not totally ignore the demands of the Deutscher Bauernverband (German Farmers' Union, DBV) for protection against EC competition.

France, on the other hand, had almost double the share of her work force in agriculture compared with Germany. And these farmers cast their votes for many parties on several points of the political spectrum. The Gaullists' task in the early years of the Fifth Republic was to win the farmers to their side, away from the center parties. French farm organizations, in addition, were splintered compared to the German Farmers' Union, which possessed a monopoly of farm representation until very recently. Although the French equivalent of the DBV, the Fédération Nationale des Syndicats d'Exploitant Agricoles (National Federation of Farmers Unions, FNSEA), did claim to speak for all farmers, it was divided internally as well as opposed by independent farm groups on the left and the right.

While German farm prices were generally the highest of the Common Market Countries, French prices were the lowest. Furthermore, German agriculture was capital-intensive, operating near the outer rim of its production-possibilities curve. French agriculture, on the other hand, had much slack in its productive capacity in the early 1960s, and French politicians and farm leaders hoped that the EC would provide new markets to justify intensive development and modernization of French farming. On all these points, France and Germany provide interesting material for comparative research.

THE COMMUNITY POLITICAL SYSTEM

The chief incentive for farmers to organize on the Community level is the Commission's rule of dealing only with Eurogroups, not with national interest groups. Since the Council of Ministers, the final decision-making body, may not take independent action (except in a small number of important areas such as the admission of new members) but must instead rule on proposals put forward by the thirteen-member Commission, this rule of granting access only to Eurogroups provides a powerful incentive to national groups for organizing on the Community level.

Eurogroups have had little success in gaining access to the Council, however. Here, the older patterns prevail: The national groups have discussed proposals with their minister at length before he boards the train in Paris or Bonn for Brussels. Hence, a dual pattern of access characterizes EC politics. Community influence strategies are most noticeable during the discussion stage when proposals are being drawn up by the Commission; at the moment of formal decision, national strategies still dominate.

The substitution of the Community decision-making system for national systems accentuated certain tendencies already evident within national systems before 1958:

1. The decline of legislative power: After 1958, decisions on the common agricultural policy were taken within the EC Council, and they could not be

changed by national legislatures. The most that a legislature could do was to
direct the national minister to pursue a certain course in Brussels. If he failed to
follow the order, he (or the national government) might be overturned by the
legislature. In any case, the Council decision retained the force of law.

2. The decline of certain farm groups' influence: Groups that may have
been important in one nation's political system found their strength greatly di-
luted in the enlarged system. This was especially true of the French reformist
group, the Centre National des Jeunes Agriculteurs (National Center of Young
Farmers, CNJA).

3. Difficulties in developing a coherent farm policy: These increased as the
national system was supplanted by the EC. National governments had trouble
coordinating positions taken by various ministers and officials in Brussels. This
caused governments to tighten the controls over national bureaucrats and ministers working on EC affairs.[3]

4. The more complex EC decision-making process: National ministers now
set farm prices and decided other questions in Brussels with little supervision by
national legislatures. This often forced national groups to work more closely
with the national executive to defend their interests in Brussels. This, in turn,
constrained their opposition to national government policies. As the president of
the German Farmers' Union put it, "If we ask members of the German government to support our position in Brussels, we cannot at the same time call them
'murderers of the farmers.' "[4] Close relations with the Agriculture Ministry and
the cabinet were now more necessary than ever.

5. The increased complexity of the policy-making process: The political
inputs of nine different systems are fed into the Commission's and the Council's
deliberations, which are often sidetracked or postponed because of national elections, riots, and so forth.

6. The increased remoteness of the EC: Community proposals emanate
from an appointed Commission and are adopted by a Council that can be challenged by no one and that has no obligation to heed the advice of any other
body.

THE POLICY AREA: AGRICULTURE

The Treaty of Rome obliged the states of the EC to establish a "common
agricultural policy," but it did not specify the content of such a policy. In contrast to the detailed timetables set down for freeing intra-Community trade in
industrial products, the field of agriculture received rather vague consideration
in the treaty. It was apparent from the beginning that agriculture could not be
included with industrial products in the liberalization of trade: The difficulties
of finding equilibrium of supply and demand, together with the existence of
entrenched national market organizations, prevented a freeing of trade in farm

products similar to that envisaged for industrial goods. The goal of the member states was rather to construct a unified policy for agriculture that would harmonize the national farm policies already operating.[5]

The Treaty of Rome set down five goals that such a common agricultural policy should pursue: increased productivity, a decent standard of living for farmers, market stabilization, security of food supplies, and reasonable prices to consumers.[6] These five goals can easily, in many circumstances, be contradictory: The assurance of good incomes to farmers seems difficult to reconcile with the stabilization of markets and reasonable prices for consumers, given the nature of European agriculture in 1958. It should also be noted that, in contrast to the German Agricultural Law of 1955 and the French Orientation Law of 1960, the treaty does not specify *parity* of farm and nonfarm incomes as one of the goals of the new policy.

The common agricultural policy has involved an effort to permit free trade in farm goods by setting suitable prices and market-intervention guidelines for the entire Community. A Farm Fund, Fonds Européen d'Orientation et de Garantie Agricole (FEOGA), administers the price and subsidy policies, as well as the structural-reform program aimed at reducing the number of farmers and modernizing operations.

The policy has experienced severe shocks since the demise of the Bretton Woods system of stable exchange rates. Community prices are set in terms of a unit of account (UA), which in turn is defined with reference to the predevaluation dollar. If member states' currencies float, complex adjustments must be made to Community farm prices as goods pass from one member state to another. These border taxes, or monetary compensation amounts (*montants compensatoires*), have in effect reintroduced national markets surrounded by tariff walls. The extreme technicality of the problem has not prevented it from becoming a serious political and economic issue for interest groups of different countries. German farmers desire the continuation of border taxes; the great strength of the mark since 1969 would otherwise make the sale of German farm products to states such as Italy extremely difficult. French farmers desire the abolition of border taxes for opposite reasons.

The common agricultural policy is, therefore, a collection of extremely complex provisions affecting European farming. The debates on whether to have common prices, the level of such prices, the financing of surpluses, and structural reform—not to mention the share of each farm product in the total Community farm budget—provide abundant subjects for dispute among national governments, political parties, and interest groups. These disputes arose within a complicated Community political system. A complex series of linkages between national political systems and the Community system meant that any given political actor had to thread his way through an institutional labyrinth. In this work we concentrate on one class of actors, interest groups, in order to see how they attempted to influence Community decisions after the integration process had changed the national systems to which they had been accustomed.

NOTES

1. Uwe Kitzinger, "Problems of a European Political Economy," in *The European Community in the 1970s*, ed. Steven Warnecke (New York: Praeger Publishers, 1972), p. 31.

2. Edward Kolodziej, *French International Policy Under de Gaulle and Pompidou* (Ithaca, N.Y.: Cornell University Press, 1974), pp. 263-74.

3. Helen Wallace, *National Governments and the European Communities* (London: Chatham House, PEP, 1973), p. 85.

4. *Agra-Europe*, February 18, 1971.

5. François Clerc, *Le Marché Commun agricole* (Paris: Presses Universitaries de France, 1965), pp. 36-37.

6. Treaty Establishing the European Economic Community, Article 39, in Eric Stein and Peter Hay, eds., *Documents for Use with Cases and Materials on the Law and Institutions of the Atlantic Area* (Ann Arbor, Mich.: Overbeck Company, 1963), p. 50.

2

**FARM POLITICS
IN GERMANY**

Agriculture has occupied a prominent place in the politics of the two nations examined in this work, Germany and France. In Germany, the great landed estates of the Junkers in Prussia provided the economic base for a class that dominated the Second Reich and continued to exercise great influence in the Weimar Republic. Only the conflagration of World War II and the total annexation of eastern Prussia by the Soviet Union and Poland finally eliminated this social class: The Third Reich's "collapse engulfed half a millennium of Junker power."[1]

Only in the early 1950s did Germany begin to consider problems of farm modernization. The introduction of the European Community's common agricultural policy was favored primarily for diplomatic and industrial reasons; it would not benefit German agriculture substantially.

In France, the peasantry often played a key role in national politics, being courted by the succession of regimes following the Revolution.

After World War II, France faced the task of modernizing her farms and reducing her farm population while avoiding excessive social tension. The introduction of the Community's common agricultural policy in the mid-1960s promised to help her in this task, though it posed new dilemmas for the government as well as the farm organizations.

In the new West German Republic of the late 1940s, the number of farmers was greatly reduced in comparison with the Germany of 1939. The establishment of the Federal Republic on the western third of the prewar Reich produced a state more heavily industrialized and more Catholic than its prewar predecessor. The importance of farmers in the work force was smaller: In 1954, only 19.7 percent of the West German work force was engaged in agriculture.[2]

The farms of West Germany were small in comparison with the great estates of the eastern plains. There had been no enclosure movement in western Germany, as there had been in eighteenth-century England. The western German farms were therefore fragmented.[3] Farmsteads were concentrated in villages and the farmer had to walk to his scattered parcels, a highly inefficient system.[4]

The bulk of German farm operations were on a modest scale. Figure 1 is a histogram on German farm units; two-thirds of them had an area of 10 hectares or less in 1959. (For France, the situation was more varied: only one-half of the farm units had an area of less than 10 hectares in 1955. About 5 percent of French farm units were larger than 50 hectares; only 1 percent of German units exceeded this size.[5]

FIGURE 1

Size Distribution of Farms in West Germany, 1959

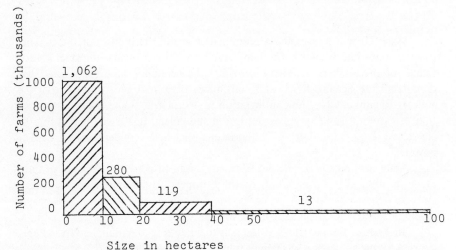

Size in hectares

Source: Office Statistique des Communautes Européennes in Yves Malgrain, *L'Integration agricole dans l'Europe des Six* (Paris: Editions Cujas, 1965), p. 50. Not shown: 2,800 farms over 100 hectares.

The primary aim of the new German government in the early 1950s was to provide cheap food to the consumer. After the currency reform of the late 1940s, food imports became expensive. The government's cheap-food policy resulted in the establishment of the Einfuhr- und Vorratstellen (Import and Stocking Boards, EVSt), set up in 1950-51. The Boards had a public monopoly on imports of cereals, fodder, livestock, meat, milk, and sugar. They paid from taxes the difference between high world prices and low prices for the German consumer.[6] During the Korean War, the German farmer was sheltered from competition from cheaper food sources.[7]

Two products in particular received guaranteed protection, grains and sugar. They remained directly controlled by the price mechanism, with the Boards purchasing all German supplies at a certain price. The prices for the other products were protected in a much looser way, by means of the Boards' purchases to firm up prices when necessary.[8]

The price-support system set up by the EC after 1962 closely resembled the activities of the EVSt bodies. The German Boards continued in existence, enforcing support rules made in Brussels. The Boards are "statutory public boards directed and controlled by the Federal Ministry of Agriculture." Each EVSt has a board of directors consisting of 24 representatives of the federal ministries of agriculture, finance, and economic affairs, the *Länder* governments, the farmers' and producers' organizations, wholesalers' and retailers' associations, processors, and consumers. The board of directors meets only two or three times a year, and nongovernment interests' participation appears nominal. This is not surprising, in light of the great diversity of interests represented and the formal representation of the finance and economic-affairs ministries in the operation of the Boards.[9]

It is interesting to note the dominance of grains in terms of overall EVSt activity: The grain EVSt has a staff almost twice as large as the combined staffs of the other Boards, about 450 in the late 1960s.[10] This was the case in spite of the fact that four-fifths of agricultural production was animal production.[11]

In those early years of the Federal Republic, the Deutscher Bauernverband (German Farmers' Union, DBV) was one of the most powerful interest groups in the nation. Founded in 1946, it was the first agricultural organization in German history to speak for all farm movements (leaving aside the Reichnahrstand, the compulsory Nazi farm group). Whereas farmers had been divided into several competing groups until the 1930s, they now formed into a single body. In this respect, they emulated workers in several other economic sectors who had renounced the diverse and competing interest groups of the prewar years in favor of single professional organizations having the advantages of unity.[12]

The DBV reflected the federalism of the new German state, being composed of regional federations from each *Land*. The most important regional federations were, and are, those of Bavaria, Lower Saxony, and Schleswig-Holstein. The DBV also includes specialized sections according to product.

The Farmers' Union claims to represent all German farmers. It is reluctant to release specific membership figures, fearing that these might show that membership is somewhat less than universal. In the mid-1950s, it was estimated that 90 percent of all German farmers belonged to the DBV.[13] The Farmers' Union naturally has sought to preserve farmers' unity in order to have the maximum possible influence vis-a-vis big industry and export interests. In the 1950s, it built the "Green Front" in the Bundestag, composed of Christian Democrat (CDU) and Free Democrat (FDP) farm deputies who would support its projects and defend its interests.[14] In 1955, the Farmers' Union scored a major victory in the passage of the *Landwirtschaftsgesetz* (Agriculture Law), which obligated the government to submit an annual "Green Report" to the Bundestag, along with a "Green Plan" outlining its program to seek certain goals such as parity of farm and nonfarm incomes.[15]

Some indication of the political strength of the DBV in the mid-1950s is the representation of the group in the Bundestag. Of the 260 CDU members in the 1953 session, 23 were officials of various farm bodies, 21 were industrialists, merchants, bankers, and artisans, and 54 were trade-union members. In the 1960s, the DBV's parliamentary influence began to wane as the number of CDU and FDP farm deputies decreased and the German government began to give more consideration to industrial and export interests when considering Community questions. And the construction of the major market regulations involved the sacrifice of German farm interests, a sacrifice that Chancellors Adenauer and Erhard were willing to make for the sake of a solid Franco-German entente.

The German farmers, in contrast to the French, have continued to be strongly identified with one political party, the CDU-CSU (Christian Socialist Union, the Bavarian partner of the CDU). Although some northern farmers, including those of Lower Saxony, are Protestant, the farm community after the war has been a solid source of support for the predominantly Catholic Christian Democrats. From the foundation of the Federal Republic to the present, the Christian Democrats received most of the farm vote. (Only 10 percent of the farmers vote Socialist.)[16] Although the relationship between the party and the farm leaders was often stormy, it was a profitable one for the farmers. Figure 2 illustrates the farm vote for the CDU-CSU from 1960 to 1973. Some farmers defected from the Christian Democrats in the late 1960s but returned to the CDU-CSU in 1973. (The main beneficiary of the 1969 defections was the neo-Nazi party, the NPD.)[17] Nevertheless, comparison with the total CDU-CSU vote shows the high level of farm support.

The German Farmers' Union was thus heavily committed to working with and for one major party, unlike its French counterparts. This posed considerable problems in 1969, when the CDU-CSU fell from power completely after a three-year coalition with the Social Democratic Party (SPD). Now the farmers would have to work with a government run by a party that had no significant farm clientele and hence little incentive to defend farm interests.

The German farm leadership in past decades had faced a dilemma: Given the fact that farmers changed parties the least often of all social groups in Germany,[18] how could they prevent the CDU from taking them for granted when it was in power? On the other hand, how could they persuade the Socialists when in power to listen to them?

In order to overcome this dilemma, farm leaders attempted to shift their members' support from the Christian Democrats after the distasteful EC farm decisions of December 1964. The German Government at that time consented to

FIGURE 2

Farmers' Support for the CDU-CSU, 1960-73

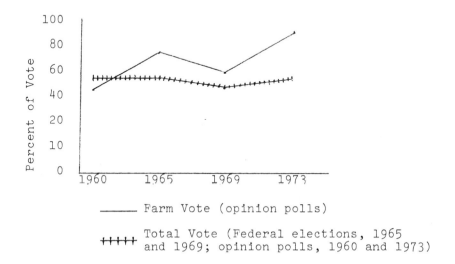

—————— Farm Vote (opinion polls)

┼┼┼┼┼ Total Vote (Federal elections, 1965
        and 1969; opinion polls, 1960 and 1973)

Sources: Hans D. Klingemann and Franz Urban Pappi, "The 1969 Bundestag Election in the Federal Republic of Germany," *Comparative Politics* 2 (July 1970): 533; Elisabeth Noelle and Erich Peter Neumann, *Jahrbuch der öffentlichen Meinung 1968-1973* (Allensbach and Bonn: Verlag für Demoskopie, 1974), p. 305.

reduce domestic grain prices in order to set a Community-wide price. German farmers would receive several years' compensation for income lost because of this first move toward a common agricultural policy. But the German farmers felt that the CDU had betrayed them, that they had been sacrificed to German industrial interests and to Franco-German relations. Further development of the common agricultural policy seemed increasingly ominous for German farming. The Farmers' Union president, Edmund Rehwinkel, began mapping a strategy to punish the CDU. A swing leftward by farm voters was unthinkable because of the political culture of rural Germany, but the rise of the neo-Nazi party (National Party of Germany, NPD) in the mid-1960s offered an alternative on the right. Rehwinkel contacted NPD leaders directly in 1966-67, and farmers began shifting from the CDU to the NPD in several regional elections. (Chapter 4 provides a fuller description of the relationship between the EC's common agricultural policy and this DBV tactic.)

The second part of the dilemma concerning relations with a Socialist government proved even more difficult. It was one thing for farmers to move farther to the right in order to warn the Christian Democrats; it was quite another matter for them to adapt to working with a Socialist government on a long-term basis.

The Farmers' Union was fortunate in the specific conditions of the Socialists' rise to power, however. The 1969 government was a coalition of Socialists and Free Democrats, the latter controlling the handful of deputies necessary to maintain the coalition's slim majority in the Bundestag. The price asked by the FDP's right wing for support of the coalition was favorable treatment on several issues, including agriculture. The post of Minister of Agriculture was accordingly given to Josef Ertl, Free Democrat from Bavaria and ardent defender of farm interests. As his official biographical note states: "Ertl was at first sceptical about the SPD-FDP coalition, and it was only after an assurance had been given during the SPD-FDP negotiations that the German farmers would not suffer as a result of revaluation* in October 1969 that he changed his mind."[19] The fortunate political necessity of a coalition permitted the Farmers' Union to establish a working relationship with the new government.

To take advantage of this possibility, however, the Farmers' Union had to select a leader who was not obnoxiously pro-CDU, hence its eventual rejection of the leading contender, Baron Otto von Feury of Bavaria, in favor of Baron Constantin Heereman von Zuydtwyck.

From 1958 to 1969, the DBV possessed a dynamic leader in the person of Edmund Rehwinkel. A Protestant and a Free Democrat, an agrarian counterpart to Adenauer, Rehwinkel also possessed the strength and outspokenness of *Der Alte*. Rehwinkel was sixty years old when he assumed the DBV presidency, and he drew on a lifetime's experience in farm affairs. He was president of the Celle Farmers' District, the State Farmers' Association of Lower Saxony, and the Chamber of Agriculture. Born in the medieval town of Celle in the broad plains of Lower Saxony, self-educated, Rehwinkel was a farmer who did not hesitate to use rough tactics when they were necessary to convince the government of the rightness of his case. Soon after his election as president of the DBV, a journalist said of Rehwinkel, "He doesn't like tactical games in corridors, but instead he prefers an open fight."[20] One observer recalls, "Rehwinkel used the fist

---

*The mention of possible losses because of revaluation refers to the decrease in German farm prices resulting from their definition in terms of the Community unit of account. If a nation revalued its national currency, national farm prices would decline unless preventive measures were taken.

instead of the glove. But often you can get more by using the glove, which is what the new president of the DBV who succeeded Rehwinkel understood."[21] The relationship between the Christian Democrats in the government and the DBV was often strained during Rehwinkel's time, and Adenauer did not hesitate to risk the farmers' wrath and demonstrations when he thought concessions unwise.

After Rehwinkel resigned in 1969, internal tension prevented the DBV from naming a new president for a full year. The organization was split between a right-wing faction—which included the Bavarians and the Schleswig-Holstein leaders—on one side and the moderates on the other. The latter urged a policy of cooperation with the new Socialist-led coalition government. For a while, Otto von Feury, President of the Bavarian Farmers' Union, seemed in the lead. But he had identified the DBV too closely with the CDU, and he refused to give up his seat as a CDU member in the Bavarian Landtag, which would have given the DBV an openly CDU politician as president during rule by the Socialists.[22] Finally a moderate, Baron Constantin Heereman von Zuydtwyck, was chosen.

The contrast between the old and new presidents seemed like a Weberian caricature. If Rehwinkel was a charismatic politician of the old school, Heereman appears to be a farm professional preferring consultation to confrontation. He was only thirty-eight years old when he was elected president of the Farmers' Union, but he traces his lineage back to Dutch nobility of the seventeenth century. A Catholic from Münster in North Rhine-Westphalia, he is university-educated. Because his presidency began at the moment when the Christian Democrats fell from power, Heereman had to call on all his talents as a conciliator in order to deal with the new Socialist-dominated government while keeping the hard-line right-wing farmers within the DBV.

The bases of DBV strength in the past two decades have changed significantly. The farmers represent a declining share of the total work force (as is true in practically all industrialized nations). In 1954 the farm labor force represented 19.7 percent of the working population; this share had dropped to 13.5 percent in 1961, and to 7.0 percent in 1972.[23] Their major adversaries in fighting for the government's support are big business, anxious to preserve the markets in the European Community for German exports and reluctant to see it weakened; labor unions, unwilling to endure continual rises in food prices; and finally consumers in general, a much more amorphous group.

However, if the DBV has experienced difficulties in the past decade because of declining bases of strength and because of its well-known partisan connections, it has also profited from the fact that it could claim to be the sole spokesman for German farmers. The Ministry of Agriculture under any government has to deal with it. In fact, the Ministry is not inclined to exploit divisions within the farm community. Commenting on the succession of part-time farmers from the DBV in 1972; a Ministry official said, "Certainly, there is potential to take advantage of divisions within the farm organizations. There might be short-term advantages to playing one group against another. But this is not wise in the long run."[24] Even if it wanted to, the German Government would have difficulty in promoting other farm groups waiting in the wings, as Paris did with regard to the reformist Centre National des Jeunes Agriculteurs in the early 1960s in order to nudge the major national farm organization toward a more progressive stance on such matters as structural reform.

The monopoly of the German Farmers' Union has, however, been shaken recently by the secession of many part-time farmers, who founded their own organization.

Part-time farming is an important characteristic of German agriculture. Originally these farms were small operations that supported an entire family. As the farms became less profitable, the farmers refused to follow the standard predictions of economists and sociologists: Instead of leaving their farms entirely and migrating to the cities, the husbands usually found jobs in light industry in the immediate vicinity while the wives, children, and grandparents continued to run the farms. This kind of holding is common in Bavaria, southern Germany, and Baden-Württemburg.[25] The importance of part-time farming has indeed been called the distinguishing mark of German agriculture.[26] The worker-peasant serves as "the medium by which the transition from a peasant to a capitalist society is performed without a wholesale derooting of the rural population or a disruption of the rural community."[27] Until recently, these part-time farmers had no separate organization to defend their interests, which sometimes diverged from those of full-time farmers.

In 1973, of the 1.3 million farms in Germany, only 512,000, or less than half, were full-time farms in which all of the operator's income came from farming. (Those full-time farms, however, covered three-quarters of the agricultural area.) Part-time farms, as might be expected, are labor-intensive and highly diversified, with most part-time farms still keeping dairy cows and pigs for personal consumption.

The representation of part-time farmers by the German Farmers' Union was not always satisfactory in the eyes of the former, and in the summer of 1972 part-time farmers in the Saar, led by W. Herrmann, W. Mohr, and Professor H. Priebe organized a part-time farmers' movement. Priebe was a professor of agricultural economics who had long been a defender of the part-time farm and a critic of the Farmers' Union as the spokesman of big farming interests. In 1969 Priebe had argued that part-time farming, far from declining, was actually spreading in Germany and that it might be "even more a *future* form for European agriculture."[28]

This movement spread to Bavaria, Baden-Württemburg, and Hesse. On September 7, 1972, these farmers founded the Deutscher Bundesverband der Landwirte im Nebenberuf (German Union of Part-Time Farmers, DBLN), with Mohr as president and Priebe as secretary-general. Priebe had long been a foe of the EC's price policy, which he charged benefited big farmers inordinately. The

Part-Time Farmers' Union attacked the EC common agricultural policy, urged direct aid to farmers, and began searching for allies outside of agriculture. One possible source was the Federal Ministry of Economics, which had frequently attacked the entire agricultural-subsidy system of Germany and the EC as too costly. In fact, the Director of the Agriculture and Food Service of the Economics Ministry had recently published an article in *Wirtschafts-Woche* arguing that agriculture cost Germany too much. This seemed certain to inflame the ongoing feud between the Agriculture Ministry and the Economics Ministry.[29]

In its constitution, the DBLN stated that it would be a "go-between" for part-time farmers in their relations with farmers' unions, trade unions, governmental bodies, and all other organizations. It refrained from setting up a formal organization for itself. Although it stated that "its activity [was] not directed against any other professional groups or organizations," it claimed that the German Farmers' Union did not adequately defend the interests of part-time farmers: "The Farmers' Union represents, in the first place, the interests of big, full-time farming; the committees for part-time farming have hardly been very active up to now. And many part-time farmers are not even members of the Farmers' Union."[30] The Part-Time Farmers' Union, in spite of its public denials, nevertheless posed a threat to the DBV's legitimacy, which had been based on its position as sole spokesman for German farmers.

DBV leaders reacted strongly to the creation of the Part-Time Farmers' Union: "an unnecessary, harmful split," and "rubbish!"[31] Agricultural observers judged that the DBV would have to be more attentive to part-time farmers' problems in order to avoid a wider split: "In any case the DBV would be well advised to concern itself a little more with problems of the majority of its members if it wishes to avoid a slow death through wider and wider divisions."[32] Specific grievances of the DBLN included discriminatory land taxation (based on the same rate as a city-dweller's instead of the farmer's tax rate) and unfair consideration by the Aussiedlung program, which consolidated farm plots on the edge of villages and offered them to farmers willing to resettle. (This last complaint reappeared in the French case, when small farmers, led by the Communist farm group, Mouvement de Défense des Exploitants Familiaux (Movement for Defense of Family Farmers, MODEF), complained that the French land-consolidation agency favored big farmers.)

The Part-Time Farmers' Union has hardly been a mass movement, and it lacks basic organizational resources. Its president for 1974, for example, was a post office employee with little time to lobby government officials or enlist new members. The DBLN does not participate in the Economics Ministry's round table (Konzertierte Aktion) talks on general goals for the economy, talks that group representatives from agriculture, labor, and industry. The Farmers' Union, on the other hand, recently won the right to participate in these discussions.[33]

Nevertheless, the mere existence of the Part-Time Farmers' Union provoked reactions from the government, as well as from the DBV. Two weeks after the DBLN's founding, Minister Ertl announced that the common agricultural policy on prices might have to be supplemented by some form of direct aid to farmers.[34] The DBLN's president, Mohr, met with DBV president Heereman on the subject of mutual cooperation; the DBV, however, seemed to desire closer supervision of the DBLN than Mohr desired.[35] The DBV statements on farm problems paid more attention to part-time farmers after 1972, but on essential points, such as the supplementing of price policy by direct aids, the DBV remained opposed to DBLN demands.

The DBLN has received some consideration here in spite of its relative weakness, because its founding was the first significant break with the DBV. Its existence continues to publicize charges that the DBV is run by and for big farmers and that its leadership is isolated from the mass membership. Indeed, some evidence indicates that the leadership purposely isolates the mass membership from current activities of the organization. W. Wehland, for example, analyzed articles on farm politics in weekly farm newspapers and found that they were more difficult to understand than the political articles in the *Frankfürter Allgemeine Zeitung*![36] The DBV leadership seemed as concerned with shaping the views of its own members as with persuading outside organizations:

> The chief difficulties of the group's leadership seem to consist less in gaining acceptance of important political goals vis-a-vis other groups; the difficulties seem, rather, to be how to arouse understanding on the part of its own members for the organization's "policy of small steps" without losing its reputation as the most important interest group representing all its members.[37]

The complexity of farm policy makes it difficult for farmers to understand; it also gives the DBV leadership a wide latitude to shape and orient members' attitudes on specific questions. The explanation of the 1968 Mansholt Plan on structural reform in the Community is a case in point. Mansholt criticized farm organizations for the poor quality of information that they transmitted to the base.* The DBV presented the Mansholt Plan to German farmers in simplistic, pejorative terms: the "destruction of the farmers," the "devilish Plan," and so on.[39] Of course, it might be pointed out that because the Mansholt Plan involved a considerable reduction in the German farm population, the DBV was not distorting members' attitudes in its explanation of the measure. But the alternatives to doing nothing in the realm of structural reform were never clearly

---

*In a speech to French farmers in 1970, Mansholt said, "Those who speak with romanticism of the family farm either don't know what they are talking about or else they're lying." (*Agra-Europe*, June 11, 1970.)

explained. Here again, the German case resembles the French one: The existence of numerous small and part-time farmers gives the national organization, run by big farmers, its political clout. Price policy is easy to understand (though the disproportionate rewards it gives to big farmers may not be exphasized). Complex structural reforms are more difficult to convey to the small farmer. Hence one finds a verbal defense of the small farmer as a weapon to be used in political maneuvers, while the real concerns of the organization lie elsewhere.[40]

Indeed, from the very beginning of the EC in 1958, the monopoly of the DBV over the farm news media permitted it to present its own views on European farm policy practically unchallenged.[41] Diversity of farm organizations in a country may inhibit the leadership's ability to define and defend a unified policy, but on the other hand it seems to produce varied sources of information and a bigger information flow to the mass membership.

In spite of the relatively low importance of agriculture in the West German economy, the DBV has maintained a close relationship with the government, especially with the Bundestag and the Ministry of Agriculture. In the late 1950s, the Green Front of farm deputies in the Bundestag assured the DBV that its voice would be heard in the lower chamber. But the development of the executive in Germany, as in many other democracies, has reduced the Bundestag's importance in recent years. The Bundestag "is less an instrument of control over an executive branch supported by a parliamentary majority and more an arena for a constant election-oriented confrontation between a large government and a large opposition party."[42] Especially since the beginning of the common agricultural policy, after 1964 the influence of the Bundestag over farm policy has greatly diminished. Key farm decisions are now taken by government ministers in the Community's Council of Ministers, with no approval required from national parliaments. In fact, West Germany is the only EC member to require the national government to inform its parliament, through its Committee on Agriculture, of decisions taken in the EC Council.

EC Council decisions, however, cannot be altered by national parliaments. The most a national parliament can do is bring down the national government, if the national political system permits this. Even if the government falls, however, the Council decision remains in force.[43]

If relations with the Bundestag have become less important since the development of the common agricultural policy, relations with the executive have become more important for a defense of DBV interests. The cabinet decides what line the German delegation will follow in the Brussels Council. The Ministry of Agriculture defends German interests in more routine matters because it dispatches its officials to the meetings of the Commission's management committees in Brussels. These management committees decide technical questions such as the value of the import levy on farm products entering the Community, and they can thus greatly affect the sales of EC farm products by permitting more or less competition from countries outside the EC.

The Ministry officials who go to Brussels for management-committee meetings remain in close contact with staff members of the DBV who work in the same technical area. Officials and DBV staff members in specific areas meet every two weeks, informally, to discuss current problems. In this way, the DBV maintains continuing access to the management committees through the Ministry officials who participate in them. Of course, the officials do not simply relay DBV demands to the management committee. The point is simply that the DBV has an opportunity to present its opinions and its data to the committee via the German officials who participate in it. France, as will be seen, has a similar consultation system by which farm groups talk to French officials before they attend management-committee meetings, but the French system is institutionalized and formal. The German Ministry of Agriculture does not desire institutional consultation, claiming that the present informal system works satisfactorily. The absence of DBV complaints about the system confirms this.[44]

There is no structured means of access of DBV leaders to the German cabinet, but usually when the DBV president requests a meeting with the Chancellor (and the president naturally reserves such a request for serious matters), the meeting is granted rather quickly. The Chancellor then can bring the matter up for discussion in the cabinet. This access has been given by Chancellor Willy Brandt, as well as by his Christian Democratic predecessors. The Chancellor also speaks from time to time at DBV annual congresses, which provides the DBV with a way of setting up a deadline for the government to take a stand on pressing problems. The invitation of the Chancellor to the congress is then the occasion for an announcement that his government should declare itself on certain issues; if and when the Chancellor appears at the congress, it is difficult for him to evade taking a stand on the questions publicized earlier.

The Ministry of Agriculture is, of course, the branch of the executive that maintains closest contact with the DBV. The Ministry is not a "classical" ministry like those of foreign affairs, justice, defense, the interior, and finance. It belongs instead to the group of ministries that are oriented very specifically toward defending a certain clientele. The German titles of the various ministries reflect this difference: The classical ministries are called "Ministry *of* . . . ," while the clientele ministries are called "Ministry *for* . . . ," thus indicating their more specific clientele orientation.[45]

In spite of its orientation toward farm interests, the Ministry reflects more of a concern in its organization for the consumer than does its French counterpart, which, in turn, reflects the relative importance of the farmer in each country.[46] Even the official titles of the German and French ministries are significant in this respect: Whereas the Paris Ministry is called the Ministry of Agriculture and Rural Development, the Bonn Ministry is called the Ministry for Food, Agriculture, and Forests.

Even though it is a clientele ministry, the Ministry of Agriculture is near the top of the scale of politically important ministries, together with those of foreign affairs, defense, the interior, finance, labor and social affairs, and transportation. As such, it is more important than such ministries as those of health, housing and planning, intra-German relations, and research and technology.[47]

Ministers of agriculture have been political figures closely connected with the Farmers' Union. In the 1950s, the Minister was usually a member of the DBV.[48] Since the founding of the Common Market, farm ministers have been Werner Schwartz (1959-65), Hermann Höcherl (1965-69), Josef Ertl (1969-   ). Schwartz was a Christian Democrat, Höcherl a CSU member, and Ertl a Free Democrat; Höcherl and Ertl are Bavarians. All three men are directly linked to farming: Schwarz lists his occupation as "farmer," and Höcherl's and Ertl's fathers were farmers. Ertl's wife is the daughter of the Federal Republic's first Minister of Agriculture.[49] The German ministers have much more technical backgrounds in agriculture than do their French counterparts for this period.

The Minister of Agriculture meets the president of the DBV frequently, about once or twice a month.[50] These meetings concern general questions of great importance, including EC policies. Lower officials also meet DBV staff members frequently. The informal consultations with DBV experts by Ministry officials who will represent Germany on the management committees have already been mentioned.

I conclude this survey of farm politics in Germany by summarizing its major characteristics:

1. German farm politics is characterized by a monolithic interest group representing all farmers with practically no challenges from dissident organizations.

2. The identification of the German farm group with one party, the Christian Democrats, guaranteed farm leaders access during the era of CDU dominance, but it also caused special problems: Under Christian Democratic rule, there was usually no other party to which the farmers would turn if the CDU leaders refused to grant farmers' requests; under Socialist rule, the identification of the farm group with the CDU forced internal changes in the group's leadership in order to permit working relationships with the new government.

3. The organizational unity of German farmers compensates somewhat for the relatively small role of agriculture in the national economy compared to that of the export-oriented industrial sector.

4. Finally, the fact that German national farm prices were among the highest in the Community in the early 1960s meant that farmers had to rely on the executive to defend their interests in Brussels when common EC prices were being set.

NOTES

1. Alexander Gerschenkron, *Bread and Democracy in Germany* (New York: Howard Fertig, 1966), p. viii.

2. François Clerc, *Le Marché Commun agricole* (Paris: Presses Universitaires de France, 1965), p. 9.

3. G. Hallett, "Agricultural Policy in West Germany," *Journal of Agricultural Economy* 19 (January 1968): 87.

4. G. Hallett, *The Social Economy of West Germany* (London: Macmillan, 1973), p. 50.

5. Yves Malgrain, *L'Intégration agricole dans l'Europe des Six* (Paris: Editions Cujas, 1965), p. 50.

6. Gustav Stolper, *The German Economy: 1870 to the Present* (New York: Harcourt, Brace & World, 1967), p. 264.

7. Ibid.

8. Ibid.

9. Michael Butterwick and Edmund Neville-Rolfe, *Agricultural Marketing and the EEC* (London: Hutchinson, 1971), pp. 41-42.

10. Ibid.

11. Organization for Economic Cooperation and Development, *Agricultural Policy in Germany* (Paris: The Organization, 1974), p. 10.

12. H. Schneider, "Les groupes de pression," *Documents* (Cologne) 21 (September-October 1966): 52-53.

13. Rupert Breitling, *Die Verbände in der Bundesrepublik* (Meisenheim: Glan, 1955), p. 34.

14. Gräfin von Bethusy-Huc, *Demokratie und Interessenpolitik* (Wiesbanden: Franz Steiner, 1962), p. 110; Andreas Leitholf, *Das Einwirken der Wirtschaftsverbände auf die Agrarmarkt-organisation der EWG* (Baden-Baden: Nomos Verlags-gesellschaft, 1971), pp. 85 ff.; Thomas Ellwein, *Das Regierungsystem der BRD* (Cologne: Westdeutscher Verlag, 1965), pp. 102 ff.

15. For the political developments leading up to the adoption of the law, see Curt Puvogel, *Der Weg zum Landwirtschaftsgesetz* (Munich: Bayerischer Landwirtschaftsverlag, 1957).

16. See the polls of the Institut für Demoskopie and the DIVO in Paul Ackermann, *Der Deutsche Bauernverband im politischen Kraftspiel der BRD* (Tubingen: J.C.B. Mohr, 1970), pp. 66-67.

17. Hans D. Klingemann and Franz Urban Pappi, "The 1969 Bundestag Election in the Federal Republic of Germany," *Comparative Politics* 2 (July 1970): 533.

18. W. Zohlnhöfer, "Parteienidentifizierung in der Bundesrepublik und in den Vereinigten Staaten," *Kölner Zeitschrift für Soziologie und Sozialpsychologie* 9 (Cologne-Opladne, 1965), p. 139, cited in Gerald Braun, "Die Rolle der Wirtschaftsverbände in agrarpolitischen Entscheidungsprozess der Europäischen Wirtschaftsgemeinschaft" (unpublished Ph.D. dissertation, Economics Department, Albert Ludwigs Universität, 1971), p. 62.

19. Federal Republic of Germany, Press and Information Office, *The German Federal Government* (Bonn, 1969), p. 27.

20. *Frankfurter Allgemeine Zeitung* cited in Günther Pacyna, *Edmund Rehwinkel: Ein Porträt* (Freudenstadt: Eurobuch-Verlag August Lutzeyer, 1969), pp. 7-8.

21. Interview, May 1974.

22. *Agra-Europe*, January 15, 1971.

23. Clerc, *Marché Commun*, p. 8; OECD, *Agricultural Policy in Germany*, p. 18.

24. Interview, January 1975.

25. Hallett, *Social Economy*, p. 49.

26. S. H. Franklin, *The European Peasantry: The Final Phase* (London: Methuen, 1969), p. 22.

27. Ibid.

28. H. Priebe, "The Family Farm in West Germany," in *Economic Problems of Agriculture in Industrial Societies*, ed, Ugo Pappi and Charles Nunn (London: Macmillan, 1969), p. 257. Emphasis in original.

29. *Agra-Europe*, September 7 and 14, 1972.

30. "Ziele des Deutschen Bundesverbandes der Landwirte im Nebenberuf, e. V.," (Deutscher Bundesverband der Landwirte im Nebenberuf, Bonn, 1972), p. 1, and "Zu den Aufgaben und Zielen des Deutschen Bundesverbandes der Landwirte im Nebenberuf, beschlossen von der 1. Generalversammlung am 27.8.1972," (Deutscher Bundesverband der Landwirte im Nebenberuf, Bonn, 1972), pp. 4-5.

31. "Eine vermeidbare Spaltung," *Deutsche Landwirtschaftliche Presse*, August 8, 1972.

32. Ibid.

33. Interviews, January 1975.

34. *Frankfurter Allgemeine Zeitung*, September 22, 1972; *Agra-Europe*, September 28, 1972.

35. *Süddeutsche Zeitung*, February 2, 1973.

36. W. Wehland, "Die Kommunikationsstrukturenprozess der Agrarpolitischen Entscheidungen," in *Die Willensbildung in der Agrarpolitik*, ed. H. G. Schlotter (Munich: BLV Verlagsgesellschaft, 1972), p. 110.

37. Heinrich Niehaus, "Aus 50 Jahren Deutscher Agrarpolitik," in *Vorträge der 23. Hochschultagung der Landwirtschaftlichen Fakultät an der Universität Bonn* (Bonn: Hiltrup, 1969), cited in Wehland, "Kommunikationsstruktur," p. 121.

38. Wehland, "Kommunikationsstruktur," pp. 112-13.

39. For an analysis of the presentation of the Mansholt Plan by the DBV to its membership, see W. Schäper, *Der Mansholt Plan im Spiegel der Agrarpresse*, Landwirtschaft Diplomarbeit (Bonn: Universität Bonn, 1970), cited in Wehland, "Kommunikationsstruktur," p. 122.

40. See Franklin, *European Peasantry*, p. 28, for Rehwinkel's comments on the political importance of the small peasantry in the DBV's strategy.

41. Ackermann, *Der Deutsche Bayernverband*, pp. 36-39.

42. Lewis Edinger, "Political Change in Germany," *Comparative Politics* 2 (July 1970): 572.

43. William Pickles, "Political Power in the EEC," *Journal of Common Market Studies* 2 (1963): 84.

44. Interviews, January 1975.

45. Friederich Nobis, *Das Bundesministerium für Erhährung, Landwirtschaft, und Forsten* (Frankfurt am Main and Bonn: Athenäum Verlag, 1966), p. 37.

46. *Agra-Europe,* September 26, 1968.

47. Nevil Johnson, *Government in the Federal Republic of Germany: The Executive at Work* (Oxford, England: Pergamon Press, 1973), p. 76.

48. Wolfgang Hirsch-Weber, "Interest Groups in the German Federal Republic," in *Interest Groups on Four Continents*, ed. Henry Ehrmann (Pittsburgh: University of Pittsburgh Press, 1958), p. 112.

49. *Wer Ist Wer*? (Frankfurt am Main: Societäts-Verlag, 1973), pp. 436, 1018.

50. Interview, January 1975.

3

FARM POLITICS
IN FRANCE

In turning our attention to the major French farm groups we find many of the same structural and environmental characteristics that characterize the German scene. In France too, the farm population is declining, and the relative contribution of agriculture to the nation's total output is diminishing. In fighting for the government's attention and favors, the farm community also faces the hostility of unions and consumers. However, because French industry does not depend as heavily on Community markets as German industry, with its highly developed export sector, French farm leaders clash less often and less openly with French industry. Several major aspects of French farm politics distinguish it strongly from the German agricultural situation.

Historically, France has sought to keep a large part of her work force on the farm. This, it was thought in the 1870's, in the early years of the Third Republic, might give stability to the political system—the peasants, with their own lands, would be won over to republican institutions and hence become immune to clerical and monarchical temptations. The republicans used the Ministry of Agriculture for this end, and both the opposition movements and the republican forces organized peasant movements.

Figure 3 gives a distribution of French farm units by surface. One-half of the units had a surface of less than 10 hectares in 1955. Compared with West Germany, a larger proportion of French farm units are of medium and large scale. While only 0.2 percent of West German farm units exceed 100 hectares, about 1 percent of French units exceed this size; that is, about five times as many French units, proportionally, as German units were bigger than 100 hectares.[1] A great part of these large farms were in the northern region of the country.

FIGURE 3

Size Distribution of Farms in France, 1955

Source: Office Statistique des Communautes Européennes in Yves Malgrain, *L'Integration agricole dans L'Europe des Six* (Paris: Editions Cujas, 1965), p. 50. Minus woods and noncultivated agricultural surfaces.

Not shown: 20,000 farms over 100 hectares.

This French policy of maintaining a large farm population had several motivations, not least of which was the avoidance of a rush toward the industrialized urban centers, putting too much strain on the economic and political system, providing extremist movements on the left with new candidates, and swelling the unemployment rolls. Even in the 1970s, it was often pointed out that, though agriculture cost the nation much, it would cost the nation more if hordes of bankrupt farmers, lacking technical skills, poured into French cities seeking new livelihoods.

The rural population in France also adhered to many more political movements than did its German counterpart. While German farmers have been mainly CDU-CSU, with some Free Democrats in the Protestant north, French farmers have reproduced more closely the political diversity of the French nation as a whole. With the exception of a lower Communist vote and a higher centrist vote, the peasants have voted as the nation generally since 1945.[2] This diversity has continued to the present, with some shifting of farm support to the Gaullist majority.[3] The farm vote has covered the political spectrum much more than has been the case in Germany. This fact, combined with the proportionally larger number of farmers, has meant that French politicians have bid for the farm vote more ostentatiously than German politicians have.

The diversity of the French farm scene is also reflected in the splintered nature of agricultural movements. After a few years of maneuvering by Socialists in the late 1940s to create a single farm federation in which the rightist traditional forces would have little say, many agricultural interest groups arose, split, and reorganized. By the 1960s, four main organizations spoke for the farm community, with different accents, to be sure. One of these organizations was the Chambers of Agriculture, a semicorporatist body; another was the national cooperative union. Strictly speaking, there were only two legitimate spokesmen for the farmers as such: the Fédération Nationale des Syndicats d'Exploitants Agricoles and the Centre National des Jeunes Agriculteurs.[4]

In addition to these "legitimate" farm groups, dissident groups have arisen frequently since 1945, a measure of the unrest in the French countryside. The Poujadists on the right experienced a sudden rise in the last year or two of the Fourth Republic, and both the right and the left enjoyed a rise in power in the mid-1960s.[5]

Among the splinter groups that arose during this period and continue to be important are the following:

1. Comité de Gueret: founded in 1953, composed of the 16 departmental federations of the FNSEA located in central France; nonpartisan; speaks for small independent farmers and tenant farmers, mainly livestock producers.[6]

2. Mouvement de Défense des Exploitants Familiaux (Movement for the Defense of Family Farmers, MODEF): founded in 1959, closely linked to the Communist Party; opposes the FNSEA and CNJA as the "official" spokesmen for French farmers, claiming that they are merely instruments of the state; speaks for small farmers; made significant gains in the late 1960s and early 1970s as the EC modernization plans provoked unrest in the member states of the Community.[7]

3. Fédération Française de l'Agriculture (French Federation of Agriculture, FFA): founded in 1969 by big, conservative farmers who criticized the French Government for not permitting French farm prices to rise after the devaluation of the franc in August 1969; the large wheat and beet farmers of the north threatened to leave the National Federation and join the FFA if the moderate leaders of the National Federation were replaced by the more extremist leftists representing the milk and beef producers of Brittany and other

poor regions; the FFA resembles the old FNSEA of the 1950s with its emphasis
on price policy to the exclusion of structural reform.[8]

4. Paysans-Travailleurs (Peasant-Workers): a left-wing group appealing to
small farmers in poor regions (especially the west); led by reformists who broke
from the CNJA and the FNSEA in the late 1960s; opposed to the "official"
farm organizations and structural measures such as the Mansholt Plan designed
to eliminate small farming;[9] a national organization was formed in 1974 to coordinate the many local cells that had been founded since 1971.[10]

5. Groupement National pour la Défense et le Développement des Entre-
prises Agricoles (National Group for the Defense and Development of Farms,
GEA): founded in 1973 by owners of big, modern farms; resulted from the government's decision in 1971 to impose on big farmers the same tax rates as those
imposed on business and industry; one important group of big farmers remained
aloof from the GEA—the wheat producers, who prefer for the time being to remain inside the FNSEA in order to have more freedom of maneuver.[11]

6. Mouvement National des Travailleurs Agricoles et Rurales (National
Movement of Agricultural and Rural Workers, MONATAR): founded in 1975
after many stock farmers seceded from the FNSEA; composed of livestock producers of the departments of the center, south, and west; leftist.[12]

It is hardly necessary to emphasize the differences in the area of farm
groups between France and Germany. The profusion of formal groups in France
(not to mention tendencies and factions within each organization) makes it difficult to keep in mind the major developments in French farm politics. Figure 4
presents these movements schematically.

Most of these dissident or extremist movements arose as the common agricultural policy was being implemented, and hence much of their wrath was
turned toward the European Community, whose policies seemed to coincide
with, if not provoke, many of the difficulties of the small and backward farmers
of France.

Thus, while the German case presents a simplified picture of a small farm
population adhering to one main political party, acting through a single farm
organization, France presents an image of extreme diversity. Still a significant
part of the work force, French farmers act through a variety of organizations,
many of which owe their existence to the difficulties of certain regions or certain farm products.

The French farm groups that will figure in this work are the FNSEA, the
CNJA, and the organizations representing wheat, beef, and milk producers. The
FNSEA is the general federation representing all French farmers. It includes
federations from all French departments, as well as specialized associations based
on specific products.

The FNSEA was founded in 1946. Because it groups so many tendencies
and so many different regions, its positions reflect numerous compromises

FIGURE 4

French Farmers' Movements

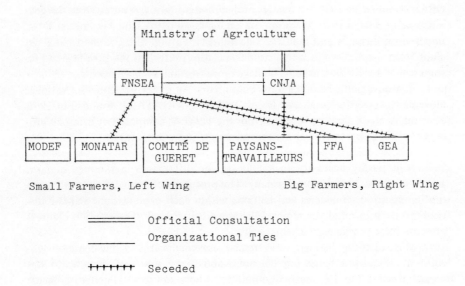

Ministry of Agriculture

FNSEA — CNJA

MODEF | MONATAR | COMITÉ DE GUERET | PAYSANS-TRAVAILLEURS | FFA | GEA

Small Farmers, Left Wing   Big Farmers, Right Wing

===== Official Consultation
_____ Organizational Ties
+++++++ Seceded

among its members. In addition, the FNSEA was dominated by the big wheat and sugar beet producers of northern France until the late 1960s. The FNSEA was closely allied with the parliamentary system of the Fourth Republic, and its leaders experienced some difficulty in adapting to the Fifth Republic, under which the Ministry of Agriculture was run by young experts eager to reform the French countryside instead of continuing with piecemeal subsidies. By the late 1960s, the FNSEA was under attack for favoring the rich wheat and sugar beet farmers at the expense of the poorer livestock farmers. Many young farmers criticized the older generation for its unwillingness to take a long-term look at the fundamental problems of French agriculture. In 1969, the reformists, operating through the CNJA, gained partial control of the FNSEA, when their leader, Michel Debatisse, became secretary-general. In late 1971, Debatisse was elected FNSEA president, after long negotiations among rival factions. Specifically, the big farmers in the northern grain-producing regions viewed Debatisee with suspicion: His early rise to prominence had been based on his advocacy of structural policies and his condemnation of the unfair advantages given to the wheat and sugar beet producers.[13]

Debatisse was the leader of the CNJA for years before taking over the FNSEA. Born in the poorest area of France, the Massif Central, he soon became a brilliant spokesman for reform in the Catholic-sponsored CNJA. It was useless, said the reformers, to continue to give piecemeal subsidies to farmers instead of guiding the adaptation of French agriculture by investment and modernization programs. The net effect of subsidies based on a product, they argued, was that the farmer directing a large-scale enterprise received thousands of francs in state aid while the small, poor family farmer received 10 francs. Finally, those products that received the largest subsidies were wheat and sugar beets, which in the early 1960s had a very low or negative elasticity of demand, while products such as beef for which France and the rest of Western Europe had a great and unsatisfied demand received little aid.[14]

The CNJA is a good example of an interest group whose status and strength were bolstered by a government to serve its administrative and political needs. When Edgar Pisani took control of the Ministry of Agriculture in 1961, he had no program of his own other than a vague desire to break out of the rut of conservative price policy that had proved so unsatisfactory.[15] French agriculture soon had to face competition in the enlarged markets of the EC. The unused potential of French agriculture promised great rewards if only French farming could be sufficiently modernized. Pisani turned to the young CNJA reformists who had already begun to offer a fresh analysis of the needs of French agriculture.[16] By conferring représentativité* on the CNJA in the early 1960s, the government promoted an ally among farm interest groups and a progressive force to counteract the staid conservatism of the FNSEA.[17]

Before mentioning the wheat, beef, and milk producers' organizations, it should be stressed that the farm-reform debates in France revolve around two phrases, "prices versus structure" and "animal versus vegetable." Both phrases refer to the patterns of opposition already mentioned briefly. The "vegetable" producers, that is, the wheat and sugar beet producers, have long received major subsidies from the French Government. Their interest groups are powerful and

---

*Représentativité is the accreditation granted by the Ministry to the group and entitling it to participate in policy discussions.

predate the National Federation. These producers have large, mechanized farms in the plains of the Paris Basin and the north of France. The "animal" producers, on the other hand, are the small farmers who raise the pigs and steers that satisfy France's growing demand for meat (few large livestock operations exist in the country). These small breeders predominate in the poorest regions of France, which are far removed from the core of the European Community represented by the Paris-Ruhr-Rotterdam triangle. Brittany, the southwest, the Massif Central—all of these regions are populated by family farmers raising half a dozen cows each and practicing polyculture for their crops.[18]

The question of prices versus structures overlaps the previous question of animal versus vegetable products. Should the government aid farmers by raising farm prices and increasing subsidies for farm products, or should it give grants directly to farmers so that they might modernize their operations? The cereals and sugar beet producers have long favored a price policy. Often the small farmers, too, supported a price policy, because structural reform usually meant, in addition to modernizing medium-sized farms, retirement grants to farmers with very small plots. In fact, the heated debates in France on the question of structural reform have been further confused by ambiguity over which farms would be modernized in order to become truly competitive and which farms would be eventually closed down or perhaps merged with other, larger operations. According to the political needs of the moment, the government has recognized the existence of "two agricultures" or "three agricultures": large capitalist agriculture, small artisan farms, and medium farms left behind by progress but capable of meeting competition if modernized.[19]

The large, efficient farmers use the high costs of production of the technically backward small farmers as an argument for high price supports. Thus the large farmers have little real interest in modernizing the great majority of French farmers. They have maintained "the fiction of a farming community" that has similar needs in all its parts. Hence their opposition to projects that would differentiate farm policy according to farm type, reducing the price hikes for large operations while administering direct income and modernization grants for small farms. For the big capitalist farms,

> . . . an agrarian policy based upon price supports and guarantees ensures a quasi-rent, or a surplus above costs, far superior to anything received by a majority of farmers. Furthermore a policy directed towards the amelioration of living conditions in rural areas conflicts in no way with the particular interests of the capitalist farmers. On the one hand, by supporting such [price]policies they achieved an apparent common purpose with the large mass of the peasantry; on the other, any success such policies might register, by helping to maintain the peasantry rather than diminish them, would, at the same time, help to sustain the peasants' electoral importance,

and by extension increase the pressure which the capitalist-led federations might bring to bear upon the various governments.[20]

The small peasantry thus provides a kind of political phalanx for big farmers dominating the FNSEA. The formation of two new organizations of big farmers in the late 1960s and the 1970s, the FFA and GEA, provides a continual warning to the FNSEA not to forsake the interests of big farming; otherwise, the FNSEA's wealthiest specialized associations such as the wheat producers might secede and join the new splinter groups.[21]

Many of the themes that ran through French farm debates in the 1950s and 1960s reappeared in the discussions of the Community's policies, especially such projects as the Mansholt Plan of 1968. The advantages and disadvantages of price policy and structural policy involved the desirable levels of farm production, the choice of products that should be encouraged, the fairness of income distribution resulting from state subsidy schemes, and the nature of regional development. The overlapping of such major questions exacerbated the European debate over the future of agriculture.

The specialized associations that compose the National Federation in France vary greatly in strength. The wheat producers' group, the Association Générale des Producteurs de Blé (General Association of Wheat Producers, AGPB) is one of the oldest farm organizations in France. Founded in 1924, it predates the FNSEA by more than two decades. In its half century of existence, the AGPB has increased its membership, financial strength, and political skills so that today it is a major influence in the development of French and Community agricultural policies.[22]

The beef and milk producers' organizations, the Fédération Nationale Bovine (National Beef Federation, FNB) and the Fédération Nationale des Producteurs de Lait (National Milk Producers' Federation, FNPL), are grouped together in the Confédération Nationale de l'Elevage (National Livestock Confederation). The Livestock Confederation receives money for its operating expenses from the Wheat Producers' Association and thus is probably sensitive to the wheat growers' opinions on the desirability of certain kinds of farm policy. Once again, it should be emphasized that the grain producers and the livestock producers are in a relationship of potential conflict: When grain prices rise, the input costs of livestock producers rise. In addition, the various measures in France during the 1960s to distribute more state aid for meat production, to the detriment of grain subsidies, highlight the significance of the financial dependence of the meat producers' interest groups on the wheat producers' organization. This financial strength of the wheat producers gives them one more means of influencing the direction of state farm policy, in addition to attempts to influence the government directly. They have a means of affecting those elites speaking for the meat producers and presenting demands to the state.

The extreme diversity of political forces within French farm politics has already been mentioned. This diversity is reflected in partisan alignments. French farmers are not identified with a single party to the extent that their German counterparts are allied with the Christian Democrats. Under the Fourth Republic, as we have already seen, farmers gave support to all major tendencies, giving somewhat less to the left than the populace in general and somewhat more to the center parties.

With the advent of the Fifth Republic, the peasants preferred the more established parties, avoiding the Gaullists, who received only 7 percent of their votes from peasant electors in 1958. In 1962, however, this had increased to 21 percent. With farmers constituting one-fifth of their national vote, the Gaullists paid close attention to farm interests in the following decade. Already, in the first few years of the Fifth Republic, the government had moved to improve agriculture in several ways.[23]

In the early 1960s, the government turned to a policy of structural reform, passing modernization laws in 1960 and 1962 that obliged the government to seek parity for farm incomes. (The lawmakers were consciously influenced by Germany's "Green Law" of 1955.)[24] Paris searched for an ally in its move toward structural reform of French agriculture; the national federation, the FNSEA, was still dominated by conservatives who stressed a high price policy, using the plight of the poor farmers to create higher rates from the government. The government decided to create its own ally. It turned to the fledgling CNJA, a group of young reform-minded farmers whose leaders had sprung from the rural Catholic Action movement of the 1950s. The government conferred *représentativité* on the CNJA, which meant that it would now be officially consulted by Paris, along with such old, well-established organizations as the FNSEA and the Chambers of Agriculture, on farm questions. The government also gave the CNJA money to train its leaders and develop strong information services to bolster its arguments in farm debates with the older groups.[25]

Slowly the Gaullists began to strengthen their farm constituency. After Charles de Gaulle was forced into a humiliating runoff in the December 1965 presidential elections, the government turned to conciliating the farmers, who had been angered by the French boycott of the EC from June 1965 to January 1966.* The success of this new policy can be gauged by the support given the

---

*Muth (*French Agriculture*, pp. 242 ff.), after examining the departmental votes, concludes that it is impossible to demonstrate that the farm vote accounted for de Gaulle's runoff. Remy ("Le Gaullisme et les Paysans," p. 246) points out that in order for the farm vote to have been crucial, more than two-thirds of the farm voters would have had to vote against de Gaulle; Remy concludes that the FNSEA action simply aggravated the unfavorable outcome of the first round of elections. De Virieu and Faure make the key point, however: Regardless of the realities, the government perceived the farm vote as the central fac-

Gaullist regime during the upheaval of 1968: The countryside remained fairly tranquil as students and workers fought against the government, and peasant support of de Gaulle was evident in the elections of June 23-30, 1968, which returned huge Gaullist majorities to the National Assembly. Farmers supported de Gaulle's successor, giving Georges Pompidou slightly more than 50 percent of their vote in the presidential elections of June 1-15, 1969 (compared with 45 percent for the entire electorate).[26]

In the last years of Pompidou's rule, the Agriculture Ministry was given to Jacques Chirac, a young, brilliant, and ambitious Gaullist who followed Edgar Faure's 1966 strategy of winning the peasantry to the majority party. Chirac, however, had to accomplish a more difficult task. In 1966 Faure had distributed electoral gifts to the farmers in piecemeal fashion. Chirac had to find some remedy for an increasingly acute problem, the widening gap between rich and poor farmers, which in large part was determined by the type of production involved. The modern farms produced wheat and sugar beets and profited most from the EC's price policy. The market-intervention systems for these products were swift and sure. The smaller and poorer farmers were generally the ones responsible for French meat and milk production. European Community prices for these products were usually less satisfactory than those for grains, and the intervention mechanisms did not guarantee the purchase of these products at the EC price. Chirac, then, had to pacify France's numerous beef and milk producers by finding better prices and intervention systems within the EC framework. Chirac succeeded in this, rather brilliantly if one considers the institutional and political constraints. He organized a Beef Office, similar to the Wheat Office that had been founded in 1936, to support beef prices through intervention buying. He pushed through the EC Council changes in Community law to permit permanent and guaranteed intervention in the beef market. He also organized a council of milk producers to stabilize the milk market.[27]

Chirac's efforts paid off in the 1973 legislative elections, when the farmers gave the Gaullists half of their votes. It was hoped that his efforts would pay off in yet another way: By early 1974, with the industrialized West, including France, sliding into a recession, the government feared a fresh outbreak of labor unrest in the style of May 1968. Again, the countryside had to be pacified to prevent a potentially explosive alliance between poor farmers and labor, an alliance that young leftist farmers such as Bernard Lambert in Brittany were attempting to build by means of the Parti Socialiste Unifié (PSU) of Pierre Mendès-France.[28]

The death of Pompidou and his replacement by Valéry Giscard d'Estaing in 1974 revealed the astuteness of Chirac's policies. Chirac had been an admirer

---

tor in de Gaulle's failure to win election on the first round and, therefore, moved quickly in January 1966 to win farm support. (De Virieu, *La Fin*, p. 49-53. Faure, *Les Paysans*, 173-74.)

of Giscard for years, and his friendship with the Finance Minister in 1972-73 helped the Agriculture Minister overcome much government resistance to his projects. In 1974, Chirac's farm clientele rallied to Giscard, who received 60 percent of the farm vote. Given the fact that Giscard beat François Mitterand by 0.8 percent, his gratitude to Chirac is understandable. (Other reasons for this gratitude included, no doubt, Chirac's role in sabotaging the candidacy of the Gaullist Chaban Delmas.) Giscard chose Chirac to be his Prime Minister, thus assuring farmers a sympathetic hearing at the very top of the government.[29]

Figures 5 and 6 present farm support for the Gaullists in the legislative and presidential elections of the Fifth Republic. The depiction of the level of farm

FIGURE 5

Farm Support of Gaullists in French Legislative Elections, 1958-73 (First Round)

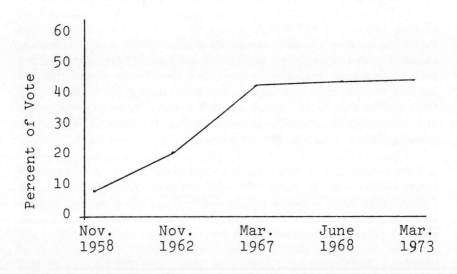

Sources: Charlot *Le Phénomène gaulliste*, p. 69; Remy, "Le Gaullisme et les Paysans," p. 264; Jeanne Labrousse, "Les Sondages et les élections de mars 1967," *Sondages* (1967): 55; Labrousse, "Les elections législatives des 23 et 30 juin 1968," *Sondages* (1968): 102; "Les elections législatives des 4 et 11 mars 1973," *Sondages* (1973): 21.

FIGURE 6

Farm Support of Gaullists in French Presidential
Elections, 1965–74

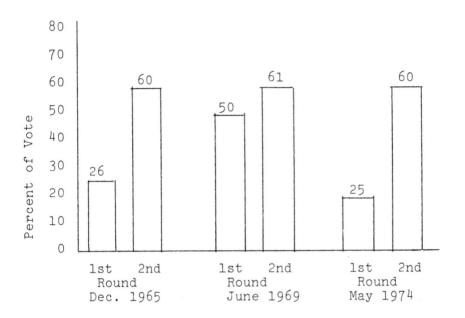

Sources: "L'Election présidentielle de décembre 1965: l'élection présidentielle et les sondages pré-électoraux," *Sondages* (1965): 25; Brulé, "L'Election présidentielle," ibid., (1969): 58; "L'Election présidentielle des 5 et 19 mai 1974," ibid., (1974): 50.

support for Gaullist candidates and Gaullist options shows the extent to which the successive governments of the Fifth Republic succeeded in building a farm constituency. The 1974 presidential election is especially interesting: Faced with the breakup of the majority in the first round, one-third of the farm voters supported Giscard, the Independent Republican, while only one-quarter of the farmers voted for the Gaullist, Chaban Delmas. In the second round, in which Giscard opposed Mitterand, the united left's candidate, almost two-thirds of the farmers supported Giscard.

The Ministry of Agriculture is a sensitive political post in France. It is by no means a political dead end. Chirac used the post as a stepping-stone to the position of Prime Minister; Faure went from the Ministry of Agriculture to the Ministry of Education. Pisani, having served the longest term of any Minister of Agriculture since World II, resigned and took a seat in the National Assembly.

The Ministry is also coming under the leadership of younger men, the so-called "enarchs," graduates from the prestigious Ecole Nationale d'Administration (ENA). Chirac is an ENA graduate. This, however, does not mean that the direction of the Ministry is apolitical and purely technocratic. It merely means that the new leaders of the Ministry had the intensive preparation in politics, economics, and law that ENA provides, which, no doubt, increases the deftness of their political maneuvers.

The Ministry also dispenses a considerable amount of money. Its share of the government budget rose steadily during the 1960s. In part, this reflected the increasing amounts of money required to cope with the adaptation of an unevenly developed farm sector to a modern economy; in part, it reflected the electoral considerations of various governments.

Finally, the politicians who become Minister of Agriculture are usually well acquainted with the men who run big agriculture in France. This, of course, is not surprising, because it is these men who control the large enterprises and who have the resources of time, money, and expertise that permit the establishment of close working relationships with government agencies intervening in the agricultural sector.

Contacts between the Ministry and French farm groups are more structured than those of their German counterparts. At the beginning of each month, representatives (usually the presidents) of the four major farm organizations, the Chambers of Agriculture, the cooperatives, the FNSEA, and the CNJA, meet with the Minister of Agriculture to discuss farm problems. In addition, on lower levels the meetings between the technical experts of the Ministry and experts of the farm organizations are also more structured than those in Germany. On questions to be discussed in the management committees of the EC, farm-group experts and Ministry experts on various product areas such as pork, cereals, beef, and milk products meet in *comités consultatifs restreints* within FORMA, the intervention agency, which ensures that the French position in one product area does not contradict the positions in other product areas. (Ministry officials then take these policy positions to the purely governmental *comité interministeriel* on EC affairs, which decides the final, official French stand to be taken in Brussels.)[30]

Only those organizations that have been recognized as representative by the government are consulted formally by the Ministry. Thus, of the various farm unions, only the FNSEA and the CNJA are admitted to the official meetings with Ministry officials. Groups such as MODEF, the FFA, the Comité de Gueret, the GEA, MONATAR, and the Paysans-Travailleurs are excluded from the formal consultation process. This, of course, denies these groups access to the meetings where vital information affecting the future of French farm policy is exchanged.

In addition to examining relations between farm groups and the legislature, the executive, and the Ministry of Agriculture, it is also necessary to examine the various market-support organizations that have arisen in France. These bodies resemble the Import and Stocking Boards (EVSts) of Germany, and some of them, such as the Wheat Office, predate the EC by several decades. They have been incorporated into the EC system of market support, but they remain French bodies. The following discussion examines the regulatory boards for wheat and other cereals, beef, and milk products.

1. The Wheat Office (Office National Interprofessionnel des Céréales, ONIC), founded by the Léon Blum government in 1936, was maintained by Vichy, which gave it its present name in 1940.[31] As the oldest intervention agency, with close links to the wheat producers' organization, controlling the buying and selling of a key crop, ONIC has rightly been called "the *fons et origo* of the French system of managed marketing."[32]

A peculiarity of the Wheat Office is the source of its budget: It is based entirely on a levy on grain producers (*taxe statistique*), which is collected by the Ministry of Finance from the licensed merchants, who in turn deduct it from their payments to producers. The Wheat Office budget in the late 1960s was $9.1 million per year.[33]

The policy of the Wheat Office influences other French intervention agencies, though no other agencies are financed by the levy on producers. The Office has received surprisingly little criticism from the traditional farmers' organizations, such as the Chambers of Agriculture and the FNSEA, partly because these organizations—plus, of course, the wheat producers' group, the AGPB—have been "closely involved in the Central Council of ONIC, and therefore have to take some responsibility for its activities."[34] This, again, is a logical consequence of the *concertation* actively pursued by the Ministry of Agriculture since the early 1960s. But this should not give the impression that they are coopted into defending a government policy that they otherwise would have condemned. On the contrary, the leaders of the AGPB seem content with the formation and direction of the wheat policy of the government. As one official stated, "We have very good relations with ONIC; the vice-president of ONIC is our president. We talk frequently with ONIC, and together we go to the Commission people to discuss cereals policy."[35] The Wheat Office relies greatly on the wheat producers' organization for information, suggestions, and cooperation in carrying out French and EC grain policy. One example of this reliance is the project to improve grain sales by instituting a quality-classification system. The Wheat Office launched this project in the 1969-70 harvest year after the AGPB had surveyed wheat growers on the feasibility of the scheme.[36]

The Wheat Office also performs an essential service for the AGPB by facilitating the dues collection of the wheat growers' interest group. The merchants licensed by ONIC to buy grains, in addition to deducting the levy to pay for ONIC's administrative expenses, also deduct a "voluntary" membership fee for the AGPB from the payments to farmers for their grain.[37] This illustrates the extremely close links between interest group, semiofficial regulatory agency, and government ministry that exists in the cereals sector in France. The Wheat Office is thus envied by the less favored majority of French farmers because of the Office's solid financial base, its effectiveness, and its close ties with the professionals in the grain sector.

2. The Fonds d'Organisation et de Régularisation des Marchés Agricoles (FORMA) were established by the 1960 Loi d'orientation aimed at modernizing French agriculture. FORMA was charged with market support for dairy, beef, and other products (but not for wheat, which remained the province of the Wheat Office). FORMA took over the functions of two boards set up by the Fourth Republic to aid beef and dairy producers.* FORMA's Conseil d'Administration is divided evenly between government officials and professional representatives: The ministries of agriculture and finance send civil servants, and the production, processing, and commercial groups send their experts.[39]

FORMA did not fulfill the hopes of the smaller farmers for a better organization of the meat and dairy markets, and they continued to press for stronger state measures. One crucial difference between FORMA and the Wheat Office after the implementation of EC regulations in their respective sectors concerns the nature of price support: For wheat, a farmer is guaranteed a certain price at the time of sale; for beef and milk, target prices are set that the intervention bodies (such as FORMA in France) attempt to meet by means of selective buying (in times of surplus production) or selling (in times of deficit). The beef and dairy farmers, in short, wanted the security of the wheat farmers in marketing their produce. They therefore lobbied for stronger market intervention.

3. The Beef Office (Office National Interprofessionnel du Bétail et de la Viande, ONIBEV) was a project whose announcement resulted from the pressure of the livestock producers during the annual Government-Professional Conference in October 1972.[40] The Office would follow EC regulations and therefore intervene to buy up beef only when market prices dropped below a certain percentage of the target price established by the Brussels Council for the year. Otherwise, the Office could intervene as it wished to avoid market disequilibrium.[41] It would not buy live animals, only carcasses.[42] Thus, the livestock producer was still not assured a permanent, directly administered minimum price, as was the wheat producer. In December 1972, Chirac convinced the Council in

---

*The milk agency, Interlait, and the meat agency, SIBEV, were "severely hampered by inadequate financing: the storage and processing facilities at their disposal, for example, were wholly insufficient to meet serious emergencies."[38]

Brussels to order permanent intervention in the beef market. Livestock producers were now assured of selling their beef to an intervention agency at any time, even if the market price had not dropped to the automatic intervention level.[43]

The Beef Office project was announced by Chirac with a veiw toward the legislative elections of 1973. In the fall of 1972 the government began preparing to create the Office by decree, instead of by law, in order to avoid parliamentary delays. By mid-1973, however, the Office, although legally created, was still looking for an address and an administrative staff. One commentator claimed that it was clearly an "electoral gadget" by which Chirac ensured farm support in the elections.[44]

4. The Milk Board (Centre National Interprofessionnel de l'Economie Laitière, CNIEL) was created in January 1974. It is fundamentally different from the wheat and beef offices. The two latter bodies are government organizations; the former is a private association that has received power from the French state to impose its decisions on milk producers if a certain percentage agree on the measures in advance.

Milk producers, as livestock producers, demanded firmer protection from the French Government as well as from the EC. They desired a guaranteed price, at the stage of production, of the same type as that enjoyed by wheat producers. Although Chirac, as Minister of Agriculture, supported the beef producers in their demand for a government body to support beef prices, he was reluctant to grant milk producers a similar organization. Any such body, if endowed with strong powers, would incur the wrath of the many inefficient dairies that, the milk producers claimed, denied them a fair price for their milk. Chirac held that a government Milk Office would be "paralyzing," and he advocated instead a board composed solely of the producers and distributors.[45] During the annual Government-Professional Conference, Prime Minister Pierre Messmer authorized a Milk Board, composed solely of private people, which would have the power to decide on minimum prices for the milk producers, as well as to set up a stabilization fund to compensate for the periodic swings in milk prices.[46]

The Milk Board's operations in the price sphere must respect the EC prices decided in Brussels. The EC Council of Ministers decides on target prices for milk, as well as intervention prices; the various intervention agencies of each member state buy or sell milk products to keep the price near the target price. They also buy up supplies when the retail price falls below the intervention price and stockpile these surpluses. The French Milk Board, in guaranteeing prices to the milk producer (through private agreement of those in the milk industry), respects the target prices decided on in Brussels.

The milk producers were not completely satisfied with the establishment of the Milk Board. It was not an official body guaranteeing Brussels prices to producers but a private association guaranteeing minimum prices that were

agreed upon by milk producers and processors. The president of the milk producers' group (the FNPL) pointed to the difficulties encountered by the Beef
Office, which was a government agency. The Milk Board seemed a sign that Paris
was trying to disengage itself from agriculture by putting the onus of price support directly upon the farmers themselves.[47]

The immediate impression one has after examining German and French
farm politics is of the greater diversity, complexity, and fluidity of the French
scene. In economic terms, the spread between farm sizes and types is much
larger in France than in Germany. The latter is characterized by small and
medium-sized farms, heavily capitalized. The former has a wide range of farm
types, ranging from modern farms in the northern plains to backward farms in
mountainous regions barely permitting their sharecropper operators to live on a
subsistence level.

The parameters of the French situation changed more frequently than the
German ones. In the most general political terms, France had many more national elections than Germany in the period covered. Even for France itself, the
period since 1958 represents a record: "Never before has France voted as frequently as under the Fifth Republic."[48] Five legislative and three presidential
elections, plus referenda on a new constitution, Algeria, the direct election of
the President of the Republic, and regional reform, taxed the Frenchman's civic
attention to the utmost. German political life seems a sea of tranquility in comparison, with only five legislative elections since 1961.

Political flux affected the French Ministry of Agriculture: France had no
fewer than nine ministers since 1960; Germany had three.* This administrative
turmoil was also reflected in the internal organizational changes of the French
Ministry. It was caused by the great demands the organizational environment
was placing on the government as it struggled to cope with the problems of a
backward agriculture gearing for the challenges of the EC market. But the turmoil also made it more difficult to adapt to the challenges, because each Minister
barely had the time to master the complex dossiers of French and EC farm
questions during his stay in office. Josef Ertl, on the other hand, has been Minister since 1969, a span of time 50 percent longer than Pisani's term, and Pisani
was considered an example of ministerial longevity in Paris.

The interest-group arenas in France and Germany show marked contrasts.
In Germany, a single organization represents all German farmers; in France, two
organizations are recognized as representative by the government, and they
put forth farmers' interests during official negotiations. A host of smaller farm
organizations, however, compete with these two "official" farm groups.

-----

*France: Rochereau, Pisani, Faure, Boulin, Duhamel, Cointat, Chirac, Marcellin,
Bonnet; Germany: Schwarz, Höcherl, Ertl.

What are the implications of having a single farm organization versus having several organizations? Obviously, the legitimacy of a unique, national farm organization is great. It alone can claim to speak for the nation's farmers. When two farm organizations exist, even if both are recognized by the government as "valid spokesmen" (*interlocuteurs valables*) in the French sense, potential still exists for competition between the two.

The government, however, has less room for maneuver when confronted with a single interest group in an economic sector. The government apparently must either negotiate with that group or not negotiate at all. There may, however, be a third alternative: The government may create a new interest group that is more congenial to its viewpoint. Whether or not a government chooses this third alternative depends on the ranking of its own goals. Does it value the unity of its farm clientele over the advantages to be gained from the creation of a more agreeable farm organization? As has been mentioned, the German Ministry of Agriculture has chosen to avoid introducing division into the farm community, which would occur if it fostered an alternative organization to the German Farmers' Union. The French Ministry under Pisani, on the other hand, valued policy change over maintenance of the status quo in farm politics. It therefore gave money, training, and access to the fledgling CNJA and built it into a strong organization, at the same time borrowing the ideas of the young reformists. After 1968, the government may have regretted its creation of a strong CNJA as it became increasingly critical of government policy in agriculture. (We shall see the same phenomenon in EC farm politics, as the European Commission at first fostered the development of the Comité des Organisations Professionnelles Agricoles and then had second thoughts about the group's increasing demands for consultation.) A government is therefore more constrained in dealing with a single interest group in a given economic sector than in dealing with several.

When a pluralistic interest-group arena is characterized by the division of the various groups into those that are officially recognized and those that are not, new elements of constraint appear for both group and government. In this case, the officially recognized organizations must walk a very thin line indeed. In order to obtain benefits for their members, they must strive for close consultation with the government. In order to prevent their leadership from being outbid by the more radical groups on the left and right, they must show that they are not pawns of the government. Furthermore, the government will not want to see "its" interest groups lose control of their mass membership under the attacks of the dissident groups. The government may, therefore, implicitly condone mass demonstrations and mild outbursts of violence on the part of the official interest groups so that its leadership can regain control of the mass. This kind of collusion between government leaders and farm leaders was evident in France in the past five years, when the National Federation's policy of consultation with the government exposed it to attacks from the right and left.

Links between interest groups and political parties create special problems if only one organization dominates farm politics. If this single interest group is openly allied with one party, as is the case with the German Farmers' Union, obvious problems arise when that party loses control of the government. In the German case, this produced internal leadership changes in the interest group, as a low-keyed technocrat replaced a vigorously partisan politician as head of the Farmers' Union. Another possible solution to such a situation would be for the interest group to promise the newly ascendant party to support it at the polls in return for favorable treatment. This assumes, however, that the political subculture of the interest-group members would permit such a transfer of allegiance; this condition did not obtain in Germany, as we have seen.

In France the two main farm groups, the National Federation and the CNJA, have not identified so closely with the Gaullists for an extended time. The government in the Fifth Republic has successfully established a strong base of farm support, but the 1965 elections demonstrated the mobility of the farm organizations' voters. And the government's sollicitude for the farmers in recent years demonstrates that it does not take their support for granted.

This concludes the examination of the patterns of farm politics in France and Germany. The major groups were discussed, along with the political institutions through which they act, especially the agricultural ministries and the market-support agencies. We now turn to an analysis of interest groups' responses to EC decision making in their economic sectors, followed by a discussion of the EC-level farm group that the major national groups have established.

NOTES

1. Yves Malgrain, *L'Integration agricole dans L'Europe des Six* (Paris, Editions Cujas, 1965), p. 50.

2. Jacques Fauvet, "Le Monde paysan et la politique," in *Les Paysans et la politique*, eds. Jacques Fauvet and Henri Mendras (Paris: Armand Colin, 1958), p. 18.

3. Michel Brulé, "Referendum d'avril et élection présidentielle de juin 1969: L'Election présidentielle," *Sondages* (1969): 58.

4. On the postwar development of French agrarian syndicalism, see Gordon Wright, *Rural Revolution in France* (Stanford, Calif.: Stanford University Press, 1964), Chapters 7-8; Marcel Faure, *Les Paysans dans la société française* (Paris: Armand Colin, 1966); Pierre Barral, *Les Agrariens français de Méline à Pisani* (Paris: Armand Colin, 1968); Hanns Peter Muth, *French Agriculture and the Political Integration of Western Europe* (Leyden, Netherlands: A. W. Sijthoff, 1970).

5. For a survey of French farm organizations in the 1960s, see: Wright, *Rural Revolution*; Faure, *Les Paysans*; Barral, *Les Agrariens*; Yves Tavernier, "Les Paysans et la politique," *Revue française de science politique* 12 (September 1962): 599-646; Tavernier, "Le Syndicalisme paysan et la Cinquième République, 1962-1965," *Revue française de science politique* 16 (October 1966): 869-912; Tavernier, *Le Syndicalisme paysan: FNSEA, CNJA* (Paris: Fondation Nationale des Sciences Politiques, 1969); François-Henri de Virieu, *La Fin d'une agriculture* (Paris: Calmann-Levy, 1967).

6. *Le Monde*, August 24, 1973.

7. Yves Tavernier, "Le M.O.D.E.F.," *Revue française de science politique* 18 (June 1968): 542-62; on the MODEF gains in the departmental elections for the Chambers of Agriculture, see *Le Monde*, May 1970.

8. *Le Monde*, December 17, 1969.

9. John Keeler, "The Political and Structural Impact of the EEC on National Interest Groups: The Case of French Agricultural Syndicalism " (Harvard University, unpublished paper, 1975), pp. 23-24.

10. Alain Giraudo, *Le Monde*, February 25, 1975.

11. Ibid., December 2-3, 1973.

12. Keeler, "Impact of EEC," p. 24.

13. *Le Monde*, October 7, 1971.

14. See Debatisse's personal reflections in *La Révolution silencieuse* (Paris, Calmann-Levy, 1963).

15. de Virieu, *La Fin*, p. 193.

16. Wright, *Rural Revolution*, 162-63.

17. The quasi-official consultation of interest groups by ministries is described in Georges Lavau, "Political Pressures by Interest Groups in France," in *Interest Groups on Four Continents*, ed. Henry Ehrmann (Pittsburgh: University of Pittsburgh Press, 1958), op. cit., pp. 82-83.

18. On the question of prices versus structural reform, see J. Klatzmann, *Les Politiques agricoles: Idées fausses et illusions* (Paris: Presses Universitaires de France, 1972), Chapter 5; Claude Servolin and Yves Tavernier, "La France: réforme de structures ou politique des prix?" in *Terre, paysans et politique*, eds. Henri Mendras and Yves Tavernier (Paris: SEDEIS, 1969), pp. 145-219; Muth, *French Agriculture*, pp. 44 ff.; Guy Quaden, *Parité pour l'agriculture et disparités entre agriculteurs* (The Hague: Martinus Nijhoff, 1973). The question of structural reform quickly develops into a discussion about regional development; for evidence on the effects of agrarian reform on French regions, see: J. Pautard, *Les Disparités régionales dans la croissance de l'agriculture française* (Paris: Gauthier-Villars, 1965); Klatzmann, *Les Politiques agricoles*, Chapter 7.

19. Yves Tavernier, "Les Paysans français et la politique," in *L'Univers politique des paysans*, eds. Yves Tavernier, Michel Gervais, and Claude Servolin (Paris: Armand Colin, 1972), p. 110.

20. S. H. Franklin, *The European Peasantry: The Final Phase* (London: Methven, 1969), p. 103.

21. *Le Monde*, December 1-3, 1973.

22. Henry Roussillon, *L'Association générale des producteurs de blé* (Paris: Fondation Nationale des Sciences Politiques, 1970), p. 19 and passim.

23. J. Charlot, *Le Phénomène gaulliste* (Paris: Fayard, 1970), p. 69, cited in Pierre Remy, "Le Gaullisme et les paysans," in Tavernier, Gervais, Servolin, *L'Universe politique*, p. 264.

24. Wright, *Rural Revolution*, pp. 164 ff.

25. Remy, "Le Gaullisme et les paysans," p. 261.

26. Remy, "Le Gaullisme et les paysans," pp. 271-72.

27. Interviews, October and December 1974; the Beef Office (ONIBEV) and the Milk Board (CNIEL) are explained later in the chapter along with the major French market-intervention agencies.

28. Lambert's attack on the entire system of state support for French agriculture is presented in his *Les Paysans dans la lutte des classes* (Paris: Editions du Seuil, 1970).

29. The 1974 election is analyzed in Roy C. Macridis, *French Politics in Transition: The Years After de Gaulle* (Cambridge, Mass.: Winthrop, 1975).

30. Interview, October 1974.

31. M. W. Butterwick, "Grain Marketing in Some Western European Countries," in D. K. Britton, *Cereals in the U.K.: Production, Marketing, and Distribution* (London: Pergamon Press, 1969), pp. 521-40.

32. Michael Butterwick and Edmund Neville-Rolfe, *Agricultural Marketing and the EEC* (London: Hutchinson, 1971), p. 44.

33. Ibid.

34. Butterwick, "Grain Marketing," p. 532.

35. Interview, September 1974.

36. Home-grown Cereals Authority, *Background to the EEC Cereal Market* (London: Home-grown Cereals Authority, 1972), p. 9.

37. Roussillon, *L'Association de blé*, pp. 66-70.

38. Wright, *Rural Revolution*, p. 133.

39. de Virieu, *La Fin*, pp. 81-82.

40. *Le Monde*, October 1 and 2, 1972.

41. Pierre LeRoy, *L'Avenir du Marché Commun agricole* (Paris: Presses Universitaires de France, 1973), p. 19.

42. *Le Monde*, October 1-2, 1972.

43. Ibid., July 28, 1973.

44. Ibid.

45. Ibid., June 10-11, 1973.

46. Ibid., July 5, 1973.

47. Ibid., January 11, 1974.

48. Philip M. Williams and Martin Harrison, *Politics and Society in de Gaulle's Republic* (New York: Anchor, 1971), p. 76.

4

NATIONAL INTEREST
GROUPS AND THE
COMMON AGRICULTURAL POLICY

The partial transfer of agricultural decision making from exclusively national arenas to the Community arena began around the mid-1960s when unified markets began to be set up. This demanded some kind of response from the national farm interest groups, for not only would the content of decisions on farm policy be appreciably different for many groups now that these decisions would be taken in the Community arena, but the decision rules themselves would be altered. The essential point is that the implementation of the common agricultural policy implied a vast change in the habits of politicians and interest-group leaders. This chapter is an attempt to explain the response of farm leaders in France and Germany as the EC set up unified markets for three products, grains, milk, and beef.

The beginning of common markets in agriculture can be traced to the Council of Ministers agreements of December 1964, when the unification of grain markets was decided on, including the harmonization of grain prices for all of the member countries. There had been earlier attempts to develop common farm prices and policies, but these had proved unsatisfying. Sicco Mansholt, the Agricultural Commissioner, in one of many projects that were to bear his name, decided to unify the grain sector in one bold move; and the six ministers of agriculture approved his proposal at the end of 1964.

Shortly after the grain agreement, common markets for beef and milk, as well as many other products, were decided on and the necessary timetables established.

These unified markets did not come into operation until several years after the initial decision to institute them. So after the wave of decisions setting up these markets came another wave of institutional changes actually permitting the markets to operate. The first concrete step toward an agricultural common market may, therefore, be considered to be the inauguration of the common grain market on July 1, 1967. In the next few years, unified markets affected more and more products, so that by 1973 about 90 percent of all agricultural production in the Community was governed by the EC system.[1]

The establishment of a single market where earlier six different national markets had existed necessitated extensive changes in market-support systems and farm groups' activities. In this chapter, the changes in French and German market mechanisms will be sketched. The reactions of major farm groups in both countries will be analyzed. Keeping in mind the relationships of these farm groups with their national governments, we will analyze their adaptation to the new common agricultural policy.

THE GRAIN MARKET

The first common-market organization, as already mentioned, was for grains. This product is a keystone in agricultural production: Not only does the most basic food come from cereals; they are also inputs into further farm production of livestock, poultry, and eggs. The organization of the cereals market, therefore, would affect not only the price the consumer paid for bread but, less directly, the prices he paid for steak, chicken, bacon, sausages, eggs, and milk. For both Germany and France, grain production was important. Although grains represent only one-tenth or one-twelfth of French and German farm production,[2] the political influence of grain farmers is great in both countries. In France, the power of the wheat growers' organization "often makes them act as the spokesmen for all agricultural interests, especially in the European domain," even though they represent only a small part of French agriculture.[3] In Germany, cereal producers predominate among the farm representatives who represent Germany in the various Community professional groups and consultative bodies.[4]

In general, interest groups whose organizational goals are satisfied in the national political system will be less interested in switching their allegiance to a supranational decision center than interest groups whose goals are unsatisfied at the national level. When one looks at the German and French farm groups at the moment of the institution of the grain market of the common agricultural policy (CAP), this hypothesis is borne out.

The German Farmers' Union by the late 1950s and early 1960s enjoyed good relations with the German Government. The 1955 Green Law had obligated the government to pursue parity between farm and nonfarm incomes and to submit a "Green Report" every year to the Bundestag outlining the progress that had been made toward this goal and the new measures that were envisaged to achieve it.[5] The farmers had good representation inside the Bundestag itself (41 deputies out of 499 in the 1961 Bundestag were farmers), and the Christian Democrats were profarmer.[6]

In the early 1960s, the DBV and the German Government opposed practically all moves toward a common market in grains. The DBV opposed such a plan because German prices, among the highest in the Community, would probably be lowered if and when a Community price were set. In addition, a change from domestic market systems to an ill-defined Community system would be full of unknown dangers: How would the market-support boards operate? What would be their obligations with regard to the purchase of excess production and the stockpiling of surpluses? For the German Government, a move toward a Community market designed to provide economic incentives to "buy European" instead of elsewhere would threaten the foreign economic policy of Germany, whereby she sold industrial goods to Argentina, Scandinavia, and Eastern Europe in return for purchases of cheap food from these countries. (Because the German farmer could not provide for all of Germany's food needs, the government encountered no resistance to this policy from its own farmers; its domestic farm arrangements satisfied the German farmer.)

Thus, the early 1960s, leading up to the final adoption of the common grains agreement of December 15, 1964, constitute a tale of German reluctance—government's as well as farmers' reluctance—to give up the security of the known for the dangers of the unknown. For example, in June 1960, the Germans opposed efforts at price harmonization in the common agricultural policy;[7] in December 1961, the Germans in the Council of Ministers opposed moving to a new stage in the CAP, because of their desire to keep an old source of imports (in this case, Denmark);[8] in November 1963, German farm representatives in COPA objected to Mansholt's proposal (which the Council of Ministers passed in December 1964) to harmonize cereals prices;[9] in April 1964, the German Government told the Council that it rejected the Mansholt grain proposal;[10] at the same time, the DBV attacked Mansholt.[11]

The German Farmers' Union was attempting to undo a diplomatic understanding between France and Germany that had been reached at the highest levels. The agreement reached between Adenauer and de Gaulle in 1958 entailed French support of Germany's eastern policy in return for German support of French aims in Europe and the Atlantic. If France decided that she wanted a common grain price, and if she gave this top priority, Bonn would have to subordinate domestic farm interests to diplomatic necessity. As it happened, Paris did not press for a common grain price until relatively late: Even in the spring of 1964, the French Government was lukewarn on the issue. By the fall of 1964, however, France chose to make the common grain price a symbolic issue, testing German "Europeanness." The American project of a multilateral nuclear force (MLF), designed to merge units of NATO states' navies in a nuclear command under U.S. control, appeared sufficiently menacing to de Gaulle in the summer of 1964 for him to search for a test of Bonn's loyalty. The unification of wheat prices in the Six, which Mansholt had proposed in 1963, provided such a test.[12]

The fact that this diplomatic goal of preserving Franco-German under-standing took priority over important political considerations is illustrated by the willingness of the CDU-CSU and the FDP to risk the farmers' displeasure by agreeing to the common wheat price, which reduced the German price from 470 DM per ton to 425 DM. From 1961 to 1964, both the CDU-CSU and the Free Democrats (partners in the coalition government) jockeyed for increased farm support, the latter in order to augment their small number in parliament, the former to obtain an absolute majority. The key promise that both partners made to the farmers was the maintenance of the German grain price. The German Government was subject to intense cross-pressures from international and do-mestic forces. When it became necessary to pursue the grain agreement, Bonn negotiated with the DBV on the compensation required for its acquiescence in the decision.[13]

Only after Chancellor Ludwig Erhard had promised Edmund Rehwinkel, president of the DBV, that German farmers would receive compensation both from the German Government and from the EC was the government able to sign the accords of December 15, 1964.[14] The German government agreed to pay its farmers 840 million DM in 1965 and 1.1 billion DM in 1966. It was agreed that in 1967, when the common prices went into effect, the EC would pay German farmers 687 million DM.[15]

The December 1964 accords were crucial in the development of the com-mon agricultural policy in particular and of the EC in general. Their main pro-visions were the following:

1. A common price for grain was set, higher than the French price (8 per-cent higher for wheat) and lower than the German price (eleven percent lower for wheat).[16] This common price would go into effect on July 1, 1967, two and one-half years ahead of the schedule laid down by the Rome Treaty. Interven-tion prices were to be derived from the basic target prices established by the Council for each harvest year, and the various marketing agencies throughout the EC would purchase all quantities of grains offered to them at the intervention price.[17]

2. A Community Farm Fund, FEOGA, was set up to guarantee the newly established common prices and orient production to areas of greatest need. After July 1, 1967, this fund would be financed by the duties levied on incoming farm goods.

3. The Commission was asked to submit proposals for handling the pro-ceeds of the agricultural levy of the Community after July 1, 1967. The question of the control of these funds was one of the sources of the constitutional con-flict that erupted in 1965, when France objected to the Commission's combined proposals on the supervision of the Farm Fund and the strengthening of the powers of the European Parliament.[18]

As can be seen, these accords had many profound implications for the future development of the Community, implications that cannot be traced here. To return to the specific question of German farmers' adaptation to this new market system, it should be noted that the DBV's acquiescence in the 1964 accords did not mean that it had renounced its policy of opposition. The DBV leaders fought a rearguard action in the two-year interval between the signing of the accords in the Council and their application in 1967.[19]

The DBV took advantage of the constitutional crisis of June 1965 to mount another offensive against the common agricultural policy. The DBV's president, Rehwinkel, wired Chancellor Erhard that if France wanted to put into question the decisions of the Six, Germany should put into question the grain agreements of December 1964. Rehwinkel did not object to French food sales in Germany, as long as German prices were not reduced.[20]

In September 1965, while de Gaulle was receiving mounting criticism from his own farmers for the French boycott of the Council, he received some unexpected support from the German farmers. In a press conference, Rehwinkel said that de Gaulle's views on supranationality were sensible: The powers of the Commission must be curbed, the Council must be strengthened, and the rule of unanimity in Council voting must be preserved. It is unwise, said Rehwinkel, for the Commission to try to accelerate the development of the common agricultural policy; it would do better to follow the slower approach advocated by COPA, an approach to which the Germans inside COPA had largely contributed. Finally, in a gesture of support for the Gaullists in France (who were preparing for presidential elections in December and meeting organized opposition by the French national farm federation), Rehwinkel urged the other five member states of the Community to buy French cereals; otherwise they would be obliged to finance the French surplus either by stockpiling it or subsidizing its export at low world prices.[21]

Rehwinkel announced the DBV's continuing opposition to the grain agreement at the COPA Extraordinary General Assembly in Amsterdam in December 1966. This meeting, attended by 500 farm delegates from the six member states, was designed to present a show of unity to the member governments in order to win favorable market organization for cereals and other products before the beginning of the market unification in July 1967. Rehwinkel, instead, opposed the application of the accords on the agreed date and proposed that they be postponed one year. Many delegates feared that the DBV would try to influence the German Government to be intransigent in the complex technical talks in the first half of 1967.[22] Rehwinkel argued that grain prices had changed since the 1964 accord, and observers saw the possibility of Germany putting these prices in question in the early months of 1967.[23]

It is time to assess the DBV's actions in terms of the hypothesis on organizational goals. Clearly, a major concern of the German Farmers' Union was the major reduction in farm prices entailed by the EC market. But market security was also important. The compensation promised by Erhard to Rehwinkel was not as satisfactory as a high grain price. And the postponement in compensation payments in the following years, in spite of Erhard's 1964 promise to Rehwinkel, demonstrated the uncertainty of such agreements. The marketing agencies, the promise of parity included in the 1955 Agricultural Law, the strong farm representation inside the parliament—all of these national relationships seemed in danger as German agriculture prepared to be incorporated into the EC.

We now turn to the French group concerned with the grain policy of the Community. This case provides an interesting contrast to the German one: Here we find a powerful special-interest group that, despite its power, had experienced difficulties in its relations with the national government during the years 1958-64. The behavior of the French wheat producers, therefore, casts an interesting light on the hypothesis about group goals because the wheat producers' organization, the AGPB, did in fact support integration in its domain of cereals production.

The downturn in the AGPB's relationships with the French Government after 1958 occurred because of three main developments: change in the nature of the regime, change in the rewards that the regulatory action of the regime could deliver, and hostility to the major foreign-policy aims of the new regime's rulers.

The first cause, the regime change, resulted from the collapse of the Fourth Republic in 1958 and the foundation of the Fifth Republic, with de Gaulle as President. This was a transition from a parliamentary regime in which the National Assembly had great power to decide distributive issues, such as farm subsidies, to a presidential regime in which much of the Assembly's power was curtailed. After a two-year interlude under Houdet and Rochereau, the Ministry of Agriculture was turned over to Edgar Pisani, a politician of the technocratic breed, determined to end short-range policies of aid to French agriculture in order to impose long-term direction. To do this, Pisani worked closely with the young reformists of the CNJA, led by Michel Debatisse. These young farmers stressed the need for structural reform as opposed to continuing a price policy that benefited mainly farmers with big yields and did little for the marginal farmer. The AGPB, representing the big farmers of northern France, naturally opposed this approach. In the early 1960s, therefore, precisely the time at which the EC in Brussels was designing the future common agricultural policy, the AGPB in France was fast becoming disenchanted with the French regime.[24]

The second reason for the weakening of the relationship between the AGPB and the French Government involved the latter's inability to continue dispensing benefits under its regulatory policy for cereals. After a few postwar years of feeble grain production, France's northern farmers modernized their operations so that by the late 1950s, the French market alone could not hope to absorb French wheat output. To continue to attempt to do so would bankrupt the Agriculture Ministry.[25] Could Brussels be persuaded to undertake this task?

The third reason for AGPB disenchantment with the French Government in the early 1960s involved the links between this powerful interest group and the new regime. One important aspect was differences in the foreign-policy preferences of de Gaulle and the Gaullist leaders, on the one hand, and the leaders of the AGPB, on the other.

The AGPB turned toward the EC for high prices because the new regime, in which the AGPB leaders found it more difficult to influence decisions, would not provide such prices.[26] In Brussels it found that it could exploit the German Government's defense of high grain prices for its own farmers in order to obtain high prices that the French Government would never grant.[27]

But if the decline in relations between interest groups and the bureaucracy in the Fifth Republic had prompted the AGPB to consider the European alternative, the AGPB soon had to turn to its relations with French political parties in order to guarantee that the final design of the grain market that the Council approved would not harm certain essential arrangements.

It is evident that the worsening of AGPB relations with the French Government, stemming from a variety of causes, occurred at the same time that the EC was attempting to formulate a new farm policy for the Six. The AGPB (whose leaders had been very "pro-European" from the beginning of the European unification movement) decided to support the development of a common agricultural policy for the new Community. At its 1962 Congress, the AGPB voted to support EC attempts to form a common grain market in spite of the risks that this might entail.[28]

The new EC grain market was, in fact, not without risks for the AGPB. The most formidable had to do with the very basis of its financial strength, and hence its ability to present its views effectively to French and eventually to Community decision makers. To understand the nature of this threat, we must briefly examine the technicalities of the French stockpiling system for grains before the EC imposed its new Community system.

Before the grain market entered into operation for the Six in 1967, French grain producers naturally followed French regulations concerning the marketing of their produce. These regulations obliged the grain producer to deliver his grain exclusively to government-licensed stocking agents (*organismes stockeurs agréés*). These stocking agents would then pay the producer the legal price for his grain.

It can be seen that these stocking organisms were thus a compulsory "bottleneck" of the entire French grain-producing network. The genius of the leaders of the AGPB consisted in their ability to persuade these stocking agents, arms of the French Government, to deduct from their payments to farmers for their grain deliveries a certain percentage, which would then be sent to the AGPB headquarters as "voluntary" membership dues.[29]

When the EC Commission drew up its proposals for the new Community system of grain marketing, it abolished all compulsory delivery schemes: Grain producers would be able to deliver their wheat to whomever they pleased, even to buyers in other countries of the Community. If this were to be approved by the Council of Ministers, the financial security of the AGPB would be gravely threatened:

> All the efforts of the AGPB consisted in setting up a dues system that takes advantage of the "bottleneck" formed by the obligatory delivery to a stocking agent after 1936 [when the Wheat Office, ONIC, was founded]. Today, the Community market organization threatens to put into question this solution, which has been so laboriously devised.[30]

Obviously the EC system would have to be changed in order to permit the continuation of the AGPB dues-collection system before the AGPB could fully accept the transition from a French to a Community grain market.

The strategy used by the AGPB to alter the Commission's proposal on grain marketing resembles that used by the DBV to retard the application of the grain price. In an editorial in the AGPB journal, *Le Producteur agricole français,* a few months before the Community grain market was due to begin operation, AGPB president Jean Deleau advocated the postponement of the market for three years unless some compromise were found on the question of stocking agents. Deleau opposed the dismantling of the French marketing system. Germany and Italy did not have such a system, he said. Because they were deficit countries as far as grain production was concerned, there was no need for government-supported stocking agents. The relatively small amounts of grain that were offered for sale had no difficulty in finding buyers, while the persistent grain surpluses of France threatened the farmers with low prices and unstable markets. Because the new Community of the Six would now be in a surplus grain position, why not extend the French marketing system to the entire EC?[31]

The discontent of the AGPB leadership with the Commission proposal was duly heeded by the French Ministry of Agriculture. Political changes in early 1966 in the Ministry now permitted the wheat growers to make their voice heard very effectively in the Council of Ministers in Brussels. Edgar Faure had replaced Pisani as Agriculture Minister in January 1966. Faure was more of a traditionalist in farm policy than Pisani. His job was to win back the farm vote, which had resulted in de Gaulle's embarrassing showing in December 1965, and to prepare for the coming legislative elections. Faure emphasized price policy and preservation of the family farm, the standard conservative position; he downgraded Pisani's attempts at structural reform. This made Faure a more than acceptable minister in the eyes of the big wheat and beet farmers of northern France. They were content to see a decline in the fortunes of those in the reformist CNJA who had advocated turning from a policy of high prices (which benefited, in fact, big farmers much more than the struggling marginal ones) to a long-range structural policy. And the big farmers, through the AGPB and the national federation, the FNSEA, had openly opposed de Gaulle's stand on the constitutional crisis that had erupted in the Community in the second half of 1965. (The CNJA, on the other hand, was much more discreet during the election.)

Faure himself was a friend of Henri Cayre, president of the sugar beet farmers' association.[32] Under the Fourth Republic, Faure had been Minister of Justice, several times Minister of Finance, Minister of Foreign Affairs, and twice Prime Minister (1952 and 1955). In addition, he had been president of the Amicale Parlementaire Agricole, the powerful farm lobby composed of rural parliamentarians in the National Assembly of the Fourth Republic.[33] Hence the French Minister of Agriculture in 1967 was from an earlier parliamentary regime that the AGPB had favored. He had close ties with big farmers and could be expected to be solicitous for big French farm interests inside the Council of Ministers in Brussels. The Commission proposal would be changed to accommodate the AGPB.

The way in which the Council of Ministers altered the Commission proposal on grain marketing was a triumph in squaring the circle, a process that the Community had to use more and more in order to reconcile the divergent interests of its member states.

The problem before the Council was this: How could the EC marketing system guarantee freedom for the grain producer to deliver his grain to whomever he pleased, while maintaining in France the compulsory delivery system that permitted the AGPB to collect "membership dues" easily and efficiently? The final proposal of the Commission adopted by the Council succeeded admirably in resolving the dilemma: Farmers in the EC could deliver their grain to any stocking agent they chose, in any nation that was an EC member, provided that the stocking agent was licensed by a member state. The original clause of the proposal giving the producer complete freedom of delivery was suppressed; instead the Six promised to avoid any discrimination in the conditions of licensing (*agrément*) of the stocking agents. The Commission would then submit further proposals to the Council to harmonize the licensing criteria throughout the Community.[34]

The AGPB, while "regretting" the end of the old system of stocking organisms in France, praised the new intervention system of the Community.[35] At its annual congress in June 1967, the organization celebrated the new Community grain market, which had fixed favorable prices for French wheat and would permit wheat producers to sell to any other member state's stocking organization if they wished (for example, French producers could sell to the German intervention bodies, which would be obliged to buy up their grains and stock them), and would protect their grains from outside competition.[36]

The fact that the EC did, in fact, dismantle to some extent the old, purely national French market system for grains must be emphasized. In many of its actions in agricultural politics, the EC has been more laissez-faire in its approach than nations such as France. The Community threatened many of the semi-corporatist institutions, such as the Wheat Office, that existed in France. As the wheat producers' president, Deleau, said on the fiftieth anniversary of the AGPB, the Wheat Office, which was founded in 1936, prepared the grain producers to become "credible interlocutors" of the state:

> The veritable contract between the [grain-producing] profession and the state, which was represented by the quantum [that is, the amount the state was obliged to buy at a certain price each year] was only possible thanks to that organization. With the Treaty of Rome and the operation of the common agricultural policy, things have evolved very much since then.[37]

Thus, though the Community, with its plethora of regulations and decisions, has about it an air of extreme state intervention, it must be emphasized that in many economic sectors—and agriculture is the chief example—its operation has involved the dismantling* of the old national relationships between economic groups and the state, with all the dangers for these groups that this implies.[38]

The AGPB did not permit any significant weakening of the Wheat Office, however. The Office remains on the political landscape. It does, of course, follow Community directives concerning prices, quality, and so forth. But it remains a French institution, still functioning in close contact with the AGPB. This accounts for the praise the latter accorded it:

> Close relations exist [between the AGPB] and ONIC, whose successive presidents since M. Patizel in 1936, MM. Barre and Canonne, have been the vice-presidents of the AGPB. Frequent cooperation is necessary between the Board of Directors of ONIC and [the AGPB] staff before the meetings of the [EC] Consultative Committee [of which Deleau, the AGPB president until 1974, was also president], which expresses to the Commission the opinions of the grain producers of the six countries. In this way, close collaboration between ONIC and the AGPB helped the establishment and operation of the Community grain market.[39]

---

*Another example of this dismantling of national projects, which cannot be examined in detail, is Pisani's plan to give state aid to groups of farmers who would decide their own production goals and take responsibility for the disposal of their produce. This program, embodied in the Orientation Laws of 1960 and 1962, was directly threatened by the EC in the late 1960s, because the national aid system could be construed as a measure that distorted competition.

ONIC is thus essential to the French grain producers, which is why they continue to support its autonomy within the EC. The French Government would never permit an EC body to assume its functions and operate directly with the French producer. A member of the French Minister of Agriculture's *cabinet*, Pierre LeRoy, has written:

> It would be unthinkable for the European Agricultural Guidance and Guarantee Fund [FEOGA] to intervene directly at the level of payment in the member states. This is why the fund relies on national organizations [such as ONIC] which serve as links and which must account to the fund for their activities in this field.[40]

The stocking boards, such as ONIC, remain in place because they might be needed some day if EC policies become unacceptable and a return to national devices becomes necessary.

A harbinger of such a move occurred in January 1974. By this time, the surplus problems of the 1960s had vanished and the EC was even blocking exports of Community wheat on the world market, whose prices now exceeded Community prices. Inflation was eating into farmers' incomes. The AGPB demanded a price increase of 8 percent, which the Council seemed unlikely to grant (in part because of German fears of an inflationary spiral).[41] After the Council on January 17 refused the increase, Deleau ominously threatened to ask "the stocking boards to obtain from the market the price increases that might be refused to the producers."[42] ONIC here operates almost as an arm of the AGPB, so it is difficult to see where the action of the private interest group ends and the action of the government body begins. Rather, we see a network of the big grain producers and bureaucrats using a variety of means—interest group, stocking board, EC Consultative Committee, COPA—to obtain the desired end.

Let us return to AGPB relations to the EC grain system in 1967. The initial support of the AGPB for the Community market in grains was due, I have argued, to the weakening of its relation with the French Government. The modification of certain crucial details of the Community's plan, however, was due to the AGPB's renewed links to the French Government, through its support of the Gaullists. We must examine both of these phases in the development of AGPB- government-EC relations.

Obviously, in order to turn away from the system offered by the French Government in the early 1960s, there had to be some alternative system toward which to turn. The Community, of course, represented just such a possibility. How and why did the Community take advantage of the potential support of the AGPB?

In its early years, the Community's institutions were floating in a political void, with little contact with the political forces of its member states. It was an affair of elites dealing in hypertechnical questions. In order for the Community to have some hope of survival, it had to sink roots into the political terrain of the member states. One way to do this was to create links with the professional, economic, and social groups in the member states. The Commission, for example, actually fostered the creation of interest groups on the Community level, hoping that this would spark a real political life for the EC. This was not the first time a bureaucratic organization had so acted. Often an administrative agency will need a "private" but professional organization to structure the clientele with which it has to deal.[43] The Commission's task was complicated by the fact that it was dealing with sovereign states that were jealous of their own relationships with economic and social groups. But here again this type of dilemma has been seen previously. For example, the Swiss federal government in the nineteenth century founded its own interest groups on the federal level in order to build its own links with the citizenry and bypass the older channels, which were jealously defended by the cantons.[44]

The Commission, therefore, was eager to build bridges to the important national groups. In agriculture, the AGPB was an extremely important group. Its support for any grain agreement was essential, given that the Germans—both the farmers and the government—were opposed to a common grain market. The Commissioner for Agriculture, Mansholt, was a political actor who understood the need for widespread support for his common agricultural policy. A prominent Socialist, he had been Minister of Agriculture in five successive cabinets in the Netherlands before joining the Commission in 1958; he was adept in dealing with the highly organized Dutch farmers. Mansholt knew that because grain was the keystone of farm policy, being an important foodstuff and an important input for other farm products, the common agricultural policy should begin with grain. In addition, he knew that a grain policy meant the agreement of the AGPB, or at least its acquiescence.[45]

The alliance between Mansholt and the Commission, on the one hand, and the AGPB, on the other, was usually tacit from 1963 to 1965, but substantial evidence nevertheless indicates that such an alliance existed. As Hélène Delorme concludes, after a careful examination of the positions taken by all parties on the proposal to unite the grain market and the grain price,

> Actually, if [the French] government had neither frozen internal farm prices for two years nor, in 1965, threatened the breakdown of the Common Market, [French] farmers would not have turned toward the Commission; but, without the comprehension and the help they found in the Commission, their action would probably have been less effective. For this reason, one may speak of a veritable alliance, though the Commission is able only with difficulty to present itself as the defender of a national group. The Commission may only support a national group discreetly in the group's action and inform the group of the Commission's version of the facts. Several pieces of evidence show that such was the attitude of the Commission during these two years.[46]

Mansholt communicated directly with the AGPB, as well as with its president, Deleau, who was at that time a member of the Praesidium of COPA, a group Mansholt consulted monthly.[47]

Mansholt had placed a senior French official in a key position on his staff to convince the conservative farm organizations of France that the Commission's agricultural policies would not be too radical. "By skillful maneuvering, Mr. Mansholt came to a kind of gentleman's agreement with the French: he would help them in the agricultural sector so long as they did not present too much opposition to certain aspects of his policies likely to be interpreted as social-ist."[48] The French grain producers, especially the wheat producers, received a formidable price increase from the December 1964 accords, though the French Government opposed a price increase because of its inflationary potential.[49] The EC wheat price was 8 percent higher than the former French price. The re-formists of the CNJA immediately attacked the price as favoring the big northern French farmers while hurting the small farmers of Brittany, the west, and the southwest, because the corn price was not increased nearly as much.[50]

Further circumstantial evidence of a bargain between Mansholt and the Commission, on the one hand, and the AGPB, on the other, comes from the position taken by Deleau through COPA on structural reform a few years later. Before the mid-1960s, the subject of structural reform was anathema to big French farmers. By changing the emphasis of farm policy from price supports, which naturally gave the biggest profits to large modern farms, to modernization plans aimed at improving the methods of marginal farmers, proponents of struc-tural reform were threatening the interests of big farmers. The latter fought the CNJA for control of the national French farm federation, the FNSEA, in the mid-1960s.[51] By 1967, however, Mansholt was preaching the virtues of struc-tural reform for the entire EC, and at the end of 1968 he announced his plan for drastic changes in European farming, involving the reduction of the farm population by half from 1970 to 1980 and a modernization program for the farmers who remained in agriculture.[52] At first sight, it appears that this Man-sholt Plan, as it came to be called, should have provoked the wrath of the AGPB, whose leaders had often defended price policy as the foundation of any sensible approach to agriculture. Instead, we find the AGPB president, Deleau, acting as a Mansholt supporter within COPA.

At the COPA General Assembly meeting at Dusseldorf in November 1967, Mansholt, Höcherl (the German Minister of Agriculture), Deleau, and Rehwinkel (president of the DBV), as well as other agricultural leaders, debated the ques-tion of structural policy as a means of complementing price policy. The commit-tee on structural, regional, and social policy was chaired by Deleau himself. Mansholt defended his structural policy; Rehwinkel, on the other hand, argued that structural policy should be secondary to a high-price policy. Deleau favored the Commission propositions on structural policy. Rehwinkel then attacked Mansholt before the Assembly in abusive terms, claiming that an EC structural policy threatened the existence of the family farm and aimed at the formation of huge collective farms, which would throw European farmers into kolkhozy. Deleau, mediating, admitted the existence of deep divisions among his committee's members. COPA itself, said Deleau, was partly to blame for recent Council deadlocks on this matter; COPA should set up a structural and regional committee to study how national structural policies could be coordinated in order to plan for an eventual Community structural policy.[53] (Deleau's stand was ineffective: at the end of the session, the COPA General Assembly formally rejected Mansholt's structural policy.)[54]

Whether or not there was an explicit quid pro quo between the two men, it is nevertheless clear that the AGPB profited from the EC grain system, that Mansholt was able to get AGPB support for this very important first step toward the CPA, and that he later received Deleau's support for the Mansholt Plan in a move that startled even the most experienced observers of Community farm politics.

In the first step of designing the unified grain market, therefore, the AGPB relationship with the French Government in the early 1960s contributed to its turning toward the European Commission as an alternative. The Commission, in addition, welcomed such support. However, at the final stage of negotiation, just before the grain market was to begin in July 1967, the support of the French Government in the Council was essential. How did the AGPB obtain such support if its relationship with the French Government continued to be weak as it was in the early 1960s?.

The answer is that the AGPB, as well as the FNSEA, had moved to increase its influence at the top levels of the Agriculture Ministry and the government in the mid-1960s, so that by 1966 a minister more receptive to their views was in control. The means by which the AGPB effected this change included the use of party-political as opposed to administrative-bureaucratic methods of action. The crisis in the Community provoked by France's boycott of the Council of Ministers after June 1965 threatened the entire Common Market, including the favorable grain accord ratified in December 1964. The open call of the FNSEA for farmers to vote against de Gaulle, and the ensuing humiliating runoff election in which de Gaulle won by a modest margin, provoked a major change in the French Government's approach to the Community and the big farmers.

Some analysts, such as Muth,[55] have concluded that it is impossible to prove that it was the swing in farm or rural votes that accounted for de Gaulle's failure to win reelection on the first round. This misses the point. What is important is that the political actors involved behaved as if they believed that the farmers' wrath was in part responsible, and these actors changed their behavior to mollify farmers' groups in the following month. As de Virieu points out, "Edgar Faure was put in charge of farmers' affairs with a very precise aim: to bring back to the majority the million and a half rural votes that were given to M. Lacanuet during the presidential election."[56] Faure replaced Pisani as Minister of Agriculture in January 1966. On January 30, 1966, the French farm organizations expressed their satisfaction after the conclusion of the Luxembourg Accords ending the French boycott of the Council. On February 16, the French Government granted an extra 130 million francs to improve animal production. On March 1, after eight months of delay, the Council of Ministers in Brussels took up its work again on the financial basis of CAP. On April 3, France increased its milk price by 7 percent, its beef price by more than 3 percent. On July 2, the French Council of Ministers ended a special tax on wheat that had been levied in October 1965. During these months, Faure publicly praised the virtues of family farms and maintained a deafening silence on the question of structural reform.[57]

The AGPB had skillfully used two spheres of action, the Community sphere and the national sphere; it had also cleverly exploited the methods of bureaucratic and partisan politics to its fullest advantage.

After reviewing the reactions of German and French farmers to the EC grain accord, and its implementation, we can make the following hypothesis: As was expected, interest groups do in fact turn to supranational institutions for satisfaction of their organizational goals when the national system is no longer able to satisfy them. But the supranational institution must be able to offer satisfying rewards; it must offer something toward which to turn. In the French case, the wheat producers looked for an alternative source of rewards in the form of higher prices, export subsidies, and surplus storage when it became clear that the French Government was no longer financially or politically capable of meeting these goals. In the German case, the German farmers were quite satisfied with the complex structure of prices, tariffs, and marketing agencies that they had built with the cooperation of major political parties and the relevant ministries. They had no incentive to abandon such a comfortable and rewarding system.

Associated with the hypothesis on interest-group reactions to integration efforts were observations on the groups' use of bureaucratic and party relationships. Far from decreasing in importance, both of these types of relationships increased in importance on the national level as groups struggled either to push through new schemes on the EC level, for which they needed the support of national bureaucracies and national government leaders, or to preserve the national support systems and foil the new EC regulations. And even when groups such as the French wheat producers wholeheartedly supported new EC regulations, they and the national civil servants in the national marketing agencies maintained control over the implementation of the EC regulations. Party politics becomes extremely important when groups shift their attention toward the EC, because it is through the top government leaders, especially the relevant minister, that these groups can secure passage of favorable decisions on the EC level through the Council of Ministers.

In sum, examination of the shift in decision making from national political systems to the EC in the grain sector has shown the supreme importance for national interest groups to retain the support of the national bureaucrats who will implement EC policy, as well as the national politicians at high government levels who shape the government's stance inside the Council on the relevant regulations.

This last point should be stressed because the political inputs of Council decisions have been overlooked in much of the research on European integration as theorists directed their attention toward the role of the Commission. Because of the EC's decision-making structure, gains promised by the Commission to national groups must be ratified by the Council. And the levers of influence on the Council are to be found in the realm of party-political action in the national arena. National votes in the Council are decided at the highest levels of government within each national system. In its struggle to influence these decisions, a national interest group must rely on its political strength to be heard. We may assume with some confidence that when de Gaulle met with his ministers at the end of December 1965 to chart the future course of French farm policy, questions of economic rationality were not uppermost in their minds. He had almost lost one election because of farmers' hostility, and he had to face another one, for the legislature, in a year. De Gaulle changed French policy to avoid political disaster.

Thus, after considering this first case of policy integration in France and Germany, we conclude that even the most propitious conditions will provoke only a partial adherence to a Community bureaucratic network. The specific decision-making structure of the EC, moreover, ensures that the crucial stage of refining proposals and balancing interests in order to come to a final decision is lodged in the Council of Ministers. And it is the national network that leads to access to the Council. Even the enactment of majority voting within the Council would not alter the fact that the fundamental source of influence inside the Council for an interest group is the network of national channels. We must therefore conclude that while the approaches to the Commission via Community-level Eurogroups are a possible means of access and influence, national channels to the Council via national interest groups and national ministries are an absolutely necessary means of trying to obtain favorable decisions from the Community.

We now turn to two additional cases of Community policy and national-interest-group response, the establishment of the beef and milk markets. In these cases, we continue to observe the dissimilarity between the French and German patterns of farm politics. In Germany, it is the DBV that fights for or against EC proposals in the beef and milk sectors. In France, the specialized associations of producers of these products attempt to defend their views within the FNSEA. And in France, regional conflicts add to the intensity of the disagreements over Community policies.

THE BEEF AND MILK MARKETS

The common beef market began operation in July 1968, the decision having been reached by the Council of Ministers on May 23, 1968.[58] In contrast to the case of the grain market, intervention in the beef market to support the common price was optional until December 1972, when the intervention system was strengthened under intense pressure from France's Agriculture Minister, Chirac.[59] Beef prices had already been unified by the Council accord of July 24, 1966. For beef as well as for milk, "the relationships of strength have evidently been determinant. The [market] organization is complete for cereals, sugar beets, fruits, and vegetables. It is much more summary for beef, eggs, poultry, or wine."[60] Both in Germany and France, livestock producers are mainly small farmers with a few head of cattle. In 1963 in France, half of the country's cattle was in herds of nine or fewer head; by 1970, this had increased to herds of 14 or fewer, owing to concentration of animals in bigger herds.[61] In Germany, 40 percent of the country's cattle was found on farms of less than 20 hectares in 1962-63; in 1968-69, this figure had risen slightly to 43 percent of the cattle.[62] The weight of these farmers inside the central farm federations of France and Germany has until recently been weaker than that of the wheat or sugar beet producers. Their condition involves not only problems of adequate prices but also the much larger questions of structural change, regional development, and environmental policy. In a highly agricultural region such as Brittany, for example, Community decisions on livestock and milk affect the viability of the region, not only the incomes of the farmers. Moreover, though beef and dairy producers were poorly organized small farmers, their production was a significant part of the Community's economy: In the early 1960s, these two sectors

> . . . represented forty-two percent of West Germany's agricultural production and thirty-two percent of France's, and since their value exceeded that of all the EEC's metalworking industries, including the automobile and ship-building industries, a great deal was at stake.[63]

For beef in particular, a rise in grain prices directly affected production costs for livestock producers. Hence the continual debates over "improving the price hierarchy," that is, the relationship between grain prices, on the one hand, and meat and milk prices, on the other.

The market organization for beef was much looser than that for cereals: An orientation price was set each year, and intervention buying aimed at supporting this price was optional when the market price dropped to 93 percent of the orientation price or less in any given region of the Community and when the market price in the Community as a whole was below 98 percent of the orientation price. If the market price in the Community as a whole fell to 93 percent of the orientation price, intervention became obligatory and the various stocking agencies in the member states began to purchase supplies of beef.[64] In addition, the orientation prices set for beef were not nearly as favorable as those set for cereals.[65]

The market organization for milk can be discussed at the same time as that for beef because it affected the same kind of farmers—small operators, poorly organized, often in peripheral regions of the Community—and because the campaigns by farmers' groups to influence these two market organizations were carried on simultaneously.

The unified milk market was established by the Council on July 29, 1968.[66] The price of milk that would be applied throughout the unified market was to be based on the price fixed by the Council in July 1966. Shortly before the establishment of the milk market in June 1968, the Commission proposed to lower this price and to freeze it for three years in order to avoid surpluses of milk and milk products, especially butter.[67] This was the situation to which the German and French producers reacted.

The German farmers' reaction to the beef and milk market organizations and their ability to influence the German Government as well as the Community institutions on this issue were deeply affected by major transformations in German politics in these years (1966-69). For during this period an interest group that had enjoyed a close relationship with the German Government rather suddenly saw the bases of this relationship transformed. After two decades of unchallenged hegemony in West German politics, the Christian Democrats were forced to share power with the Socialists in 1966. This, of course, altered the array of economic interests that the German Government considered paramount. The farmers, already a minority in the German economy, now faced a government controlled in part by the Socialists, who had never made a serious claim to defending the interest of the farm community. Where could the farmers move, on the political spectrum, in order to find a party willing to fight for their interests? The farmers were unable to move toward the SPD; their political past simply did not permit such a move. And the Christian Democrats under Erhard had already shown that they would break the most solemn of promises* to farm leaders when this seemed necessary.[68] For a time, the leadership of the DBV flirted with a new possibility, the neo-Nazi party (NPD) of Adolf von Thadden. Shortly afterward, however, the DBV underwent a change in its leadership: Rehwinkel resigned, and the new president, Heereman, who eventually emerged

---

*For example, take the story of the fate of "Rehwinkel's billion marks," promised by Erhard in November 1964, in compensation for losses entailed by the common EC grain price. In December 1965 the government postponed payment of 380 million marks for two years.

after a year of internal maneuvering decided to develop a different defense strategy.

The defense of the farmers' interests by the right wing of the Free Democrats was explained in Chapter 2. The Socialists gave the post of Minister of Agriculture to the FDP as part of the coalition agreement of 1969. With Ertl as Agriculture Minister, the Socialists abandoned their policy of encouraging small farmers to leave the land.[69]

The ongoing relations with the bureaucracy, especially with the Ministry of Agriculture, continued. As one official of the Ministry put it:

> No government can ever utterly ignore an entire economic sector. So that even when the Socialists were the dominant party in the government, after 1969, they still had to show that they were looking after German farm interests to some extent—even though they had no illusions of capturing German farm votes to any great extent.[70]

Thus the DBV leadership after 1969 was, nevertheless, able to cope with the changed political environment in which it had to operate.

The DBV was not enthusiastic about these new accords on milk and beef. The essential problem remained. While Community spokesmen in Brussels and French farm leaders in Paris might extol the virtues of European unity, for the DBV this meant the prospect of lower prices and lower incomes for farmers in Germany. The December 1964 accord had already lowered the prices of German grains beginning 1967. Now, other products had to come under the control of Brussels—milk, beef, sugar, and so on. On none of these items (except perhaps sugar) did the DBV entertain hopes that the new EC prices would equal the old German ones. "The construction of Europe" seemed to hold nothing but sacrifices that would benefit others—German industrialists anxious to ensure their sales to grain- or beef-producing countries in Scandinavia, Eastern Europe, or Latin America; French farmers ready to invade the German market; Socialists anxious to see food costs decline in order to curry favor with the urban workers.

The actions of the DBV in the years 1966-68 show its lack of enthusiasm for the new EC market organizations for milk and beef. At the beginning of 1966 two main issues dominated German farm politics, both of course stemming from the development of CAP. On the question of milk and beef organization, it was clear that the German milk subsidy would not survive the new EC accords. And farmers wanted higher orientation prices for beef. Complicating this problem was the possibility of the Commission's changing the milk-beef price ratio in order to induce farmers to shift from milk to beef production. But if this were done, what would be used to support the income of the milk producers?[71]

The second issue in 1966 concerned the fate of the compensation stemming from Erhard's promise to Rehwinkel in November 1964. The German government at this time was making several economy moves to stem inflation, and the 1965 adaptation law granting the compensation funds to the German farmers did not survive the budget cutting. At the end of 1965, the 380 million DM for compensation funds was postponed two years. On Decmeber 10, 1965, Höcherl, the Minister of Agriculture, attending the DBV General Assembly, agreed publicly with Rehwinkel's denunciation of the bad faith of the German government. Höcherl announced he would form an "observation service" to screen prices received by farmers for their produce, in order to show that they were not the cause of high retail food prices.[72]

These difficulties reinforced each other: The German government could not afford further national subsidies, because of its economy moves. Hence, it had to have higher prices if farm income was even to remain at the 1965 level. (There was little question of an increase.) This meant that German ministers in Brussels would have very little maneuvering room and that more compromises such as the December 1964 grain accord would be out of the question—German farmers would not endure substantial price cuts in milk and beef. Yet, with higher prices for milk, in which the Community was already self-sufficient, went the danger of surpluses, which the German Government would have to finance through the operation of the EC Farm Fund:

> The establishment of common price levels [in the EC], which has been accompanied by many crises, has led to the following situation: Price levels for most products in countries exporting farm products, such as France and the Netherlands, have been raised, and the transferral of financial responsibility to the EC has caused the mobilization of production potential, especially in France. On the other hand, in the other countries [of the EC] it has led not to a fall in production but rather—at the most—to a reduction in [farm] incomes, especially in the French Republic.[73]

This was especially true of a few products such as milk.[74] France was the greatest milk producer in the EC and also the producer with the greatest potential for expanding milk production: Already from 1960 to 1965 73 percent of the total increase in production by the EC occurred in France; Germany's potential for increased production was low.[75]

The DBV and Höcherl cooperated to mobilize public opinion and swing the reluctant ministers in Bonn to their side in favor of higher milk and beef prices. The clumsy handling of the Green Report by the Minister of Economy helped the farmers' cause: The Economics Ministry demanded that for political reasons the parity gap mentioned in the Green Report between farm and non-farm incomes be brought below 30 percent by statistical juggling. After much manipulation, the authors of the report succeeded in reducing the gap to 22 percent. (If they had not renounced the statistical methods normally used in the past, the gap would have been quite large—31 percent, compared to 21 percent for the previous year.)[76]

The DBV prepared to demolish the flimsy conclusions of the Green Report; it marshaled its forces in the Bundestag, which debated the agricultural situation every year after the official presentation of the Green Report. The DBV demanded that the common cereals price, to be applied in mid-1967 according to the terms of the December 1964 accord, be postponed to 1970 if German milk and beef demands were not satisfied. Höcherl in the meantime threatened to resign if satisfactory action on these two products was not taken in Brussels. The agricultural specialists in the CDU-CSU and FDP met with Chancellor Erhard, who finally agreed to keep the German national milk subsidy until 1970. The CDU and the FDP positions during the farm debate in the Bundestag in March were practically identical to that of the DBV: The common grain price application in July 1967 "presupposed" the satisfactory organization of other products by the EC. As a final blow to the government, the Green Report was unanimously rejected by all parties in the Bundestag, including the Socialists, largely because of its flimsy calculations on parity.[77]

At its Godesberg meeting at the end of March 1966, the DBV was gloomy about the state of CAP. And its confidence in the Erhard government was scarcely greater. The history of the adaptation law of 1965 had shown the government's willingness to renege on its promise to Rehwinkel at the end of 1964 in order to please industrial interests.[78]

The Chancellor met the key ministers of the cabinet before the Council of Ministers session in Brussels in mid-May. Present at the meeting with Erhard were the ministers of agriculture, economics, and finance, and the Secretary of State for Foreign Affairs, as well as the agricultural experts of the coalition parties (CDU-CSU and FDP). One may conclude that at this meeting, the farmers' wishes were not followed, because Germany agreed to speeding up the transitional period for milk and beef, as well as the mechanics of the stabilization and guarantee fund, at the Council of Ministers session on May 11, 1966.[79]

This accord, in fact, had great significance: it resolved the question of financing the common agricultural policy, an issue that had triggered the French boycott of the EC from June 1965 to January 1966.[80]

The DBV criticized the May 11 accord, charging that the Erhard government was ready to make any sacrifice of German farm interests in order to please the industrialists. The acceleration of the application of the common agricultural policy would simply bring closer the date on which German farm prices—and farm income—would be cut. In addition, crucial decisions on milk, sugar, and beef market regulations had not been made; and specific milk and beef prices had not yet been set. Nor had a revision of the cereals prices been accomplished. Faced with this unsatisfactory outcome of the EC Council, Rehwinkel said that the DBV would have to reconsider whether the parties of the government coalition were worthy of the farmers' continued confidence and support.[81]

On the other hand, the German Government expressed its satisfaction with the accord, as did the CDU-CSU and FDP leaders and industry representatives.[82]

The central beef and milk questions were finally settled by the Council of Ministers during its session of July 24-26, 1966. The common milk and beef prices would go into effect on April 1, 1968. Germany succeeded in obtaining a fairly high milk price (in alliance with Belgium against the Netherlands). The price was, in fact, equal to the German national price. Germany also won the concession that the milk price would be subject to revision before it went into effect on April 1, 1968. On beef, there was no discord among the Six: High prices were fixed in the hope of encouraging beef production in the Community and thus meeting its increasing demand.

The DBV, however, was not content. It doubted that farmers in Germany would profit from the new common prices in view of rising production costs; on the other hand, these prices were liable to cause rising consumer prices, which would, of course, lead to charges that the farmers were being pampered by the EC.[83]

Rehwinkel now moved to attack the government coalition directly. As already mentioned, the farmers' vote was not very mobile. Farmers would not vote Socialist in any foreseeable circumstances.[84] Where could they throw their votes in order to punish the ruling CDU-CSU and FDP? A rightward swing was the only feasible move, and at this moment the newly founded neo-Nazi party, the NPD, was meeting surprising success. From its foundation in November 1964 to June 1966, the number of its members rose from 473 to 18,363. In the federal elections of 1965, it received 2 percent of the votes. In its first *Land* election in Hamburg, it received 4 percent. Led by Fritz Thielen, an old-line conservative, its vice-president was Adolf von Thadden, descendant of a great Junker family of Pomerania. (In 1967, the more extremist Thadden ousted Thielen from the presidency and seized it himself.)[85] In November 1966 (when the coalition government of Erhard was already near collapse), the NPD scored impressive gains in *Land* elections in Hesse and Bavaria, seriously menacing the strength of the Free Democrats.[86]

Rehwinkel began to make contact with NPD leaders, whose party already had received a favorable reception among farmers, especially those in the south. In December 1966, Rehwinkel invited Thielen and Thadden to his farm in Celle, Lower Saxony, to "inform" him on NPD policy. This move toward the extreme right was caused by the unrest of the farmers, especially of the old guard, over the evolution of CAP and the attitude taken by the CDU-CSU and the FDP.[87]

By this time, however, the Erhard government had fallen, after the FDP had withdrawn from the coalition on October 27, Erhard's strength had been sapped from within to some extent; his CDU colleagues had lost faith in him, and "within a short time [after the 1965 elections] economic difficulties began to dim his reputation and make his placid aversion to change look foolishly optimistic."[88] The new government of Kurt Kiesinger resulted from the Grand Coalition of the CDU-CSU and the SPD. The new government was especially important for farm groups in Germany for several reasons:

First, the new Kiesinger government was the first government of the Federal Republic in which the Socialists participated. Prolabor, the SPD had no major farm clientele, except for some extremely poor peasants.[89] Therefore, it was more concerned about low food prices for the urban workers than high prices for the farmers.

Along with the rise in Socialist strength went the decline in CDU-CSU strength. The fears of those who, in 1966, had said that only the Socialists could profit from the Grand Coalition proved correct in 1969, when the CDU-CSU fell from power completely. This was the beginning of the decline of the party that had governed Germany for two decades, a party to which the DBV had the closest links. With its decline, the problem of adapting DBV strategies to exert influence in Bonn (and hence in Brussels) became acute.

Finally, these government changes meant that during the difficult period of adapting German agriculture to a common policy for the Six, the farmers would have a less sympathetic hearing in Bonn and hence more difficulty in defending their interests in Brussels.

The DBV continued to fight for high prices in Brussels up to the final establishment of the common milk and beef prices in the summer of 1968, when they went into effect. And even though prices for these products did not involve losses for German producers, the DBV remained lukewarm to the very principle of EC market organization for these products.

This case of DBV reaction to these two product markets in the Community points up even further the extreme unlikelihood of transferring interest-group support from the national to the supranational system. Even when EC policies involved no loss of income, as was the case with milk and beef initially, the farmers' group in Germany did not support the new regulations. It seems that great rewards indeed are necessary to buy an interest group's support of policy integration in its economic sector, as was the case with the French wheat producers. Otherwise, it is not worthwhile for a group to consent to the transfer of agricultural decision making from the national system, where interest groups have long used the levers of power, to a supranational system in which new institutions must be used and in which the number of political actors, governmental and nongovernmental, is much larger.

The milk and beef producers in France have their own specialized associations, the Fédération Nationale des Producteurs de Lait (FNPL) and the Fédération Nationale Bovine (FNB). These associations are weak; they lack organizational resources. Their constituencies are small farmers; their finances are meager. They are unable to represent milk and beef farmers as effectively as organizations such as the wheat producers' or the sugar beet producers' groups, which, though representing a smaller number of farmers, possess much greater resources.

Milk and beef represented almost half of French agricultural revenues in the late 1960s.[90] The price of milk in particular is important for these small farmers because milk production can continue all year, thus bringing in regular revenue. Any attempt to cut milk prices, such as the Commission's ill-fated proposal of April 1968, which does not immediately compensate by other temporary means of income support spells serious economic hardship for these farmers.[91]

Small milk and beef farmers are numerous in the poor regions of France such as Brittany, the southwest, and the Massif Central. Thus Community organization of the milk and beef sectors inevitably affects French national policy on regional development and environmental planning. And for Brittany in particular, difficulties in these sectors are feared by Paris because of the fuel they provide for Breton nationalism. (The same apprehension about Breton separatism holds for the national French farm groups, such as the FNSEA, which have to contend with very activist and rebellious regional federations in Brittany.)

The interest groups of the milk and beef producers, the FNPL and the FNB, are members of the general French farm federation, the FNSEA. (This national federation, it will be remembered, contains departmental federations.) But the interests of the milk and beef producers are also defended by the young reformists of the CNJA who argue for a fundamental reform of French agriculture in order to make it more competitive.

The reaction of the French milk and beef organizations to the Community moves in their sectors was decidedly ambivalent. The beef producers in France provided all of the country's needs, whereas the producers in Germany satisfied only one-fifth of the German demand for beef; therefore, there was great potential for French beef producers in the Community market.[92] Furthermore, there was much "slack" in French beef production in terms of productivity: Whereas Germany, Belgium and the Netherlands seemed to be reaching the outer limits of their productivity in the late 1950s, France still had much room for modernization.[93]

And yet French beef producers objected to several things about the Community beef market: Prices seemed set too low in comparison with the extremely high prices given to the grain producers in the December 1964 accords. The intervention system for beef was more lax than that for grains, which offered iron-bound protection and guarantees of a given price level. Furthermore, a particularly thorny question concerned the degree of access to Community markets that would be given to Latin American, especially Argentine, beef. (Here, German industrial and consumer interests came into play: Germany desired the continuation of cheap beef imports from Argentina and Eastern Europe, which obviously could reduce French exports to other Community member states.)[94]

The French milk producers were also uneasy about the EC market. They recognized the need to find foreign markets for their produce; yet they feared competition from other Community members, especially the Dutch. Furthermore, unlike the situation in the beef sector, there was no readily available market in the rest of the Community for milk products. For example, Germany was the major butter producer and also a major producer of powdered milk. The French producers accused the Community of setting milk prices that did not correspond to the economic facts of life for milk producers; furthermore, the Commission's surprise proposal in April 1968 to lower the Community price without any corresponding compensation for milk producers seemed to indicate a complete lack of understanding of farm conditions. So the FNPL continued to fight for high milk prices in the Community with no immediate cut in production; it made these claims, however, with a distinct lack of enthusiasm for the new market organization.[95]

The French case on milk and beef confirms the finding in the German case: Even with mediocre relationships on the national level, interest-group support for the EC moves in these sectors was definitely lukewarm. The EC provided neither satisfactory prices nor secure marketing arrangements.

In conclusion, we have found that for the German and French sides of three product areas, only the French grain producers may be said to have significantly transferred their allegiance to the new Community mechanisms in their market sector. And this transfer of attention and support was only effected after the previous national links between the wheat producers and the semiofficial market organisms in France, which assured the financial base of the wheat producers' interest group, had been preserved.

We can conclude that farm interest groups will transfer their allegiance to the EC programs in their sectors not solely because their national governments can no longer satisfy their demands. This is a necessary but not a sufficient cause. In addition, the EC must be able to offer regulation of their sector that represents substantial rewards—greater than those already available. And the new market mechanisms must not threaten any crucial ties with the national government or its semigovernmental agencies, such as the AGPB had with the French stocking agents. These requirements are, of course, extremely demanding, which perhaps explains why the farm organizations in France and Germany did not hestitate to call for national measures once more after the monetary disturbances beginning in 1969 had made the common agricultural policy increasingly difficult to administer.

This chapter has examined French and German farmers' reactions to the organization of the market for three specific products. The next chapter will examine the attempt by the major farm groups of the Six (and later the Nine) to influence EC decisions on the EC level. This refers to the establishment and operation of the Eurogroup COPA, which was founded almost simultaneously with the European Economic Community (EEC) itself in 1958. By looking at the way in which COPA was institutionalized—its formal organization, its membership, its resources, and its relations with the major EC institutions—we may find still another response of the national farm groups to the partial transfer of decision making in their economic sectors from a purely national to a supranational arena.

NOTES

1. Pierre LeRoy, *L'Avenir du Marché Commun agricole* (Paris: Presses Universitaires de France, 1973), p. 28.

2. Federal Republic of Germany, Deutscher Bundestag, *Agrarbericht 1972 der Bundesregierung, Materialband* (Bonn, 1972), p. 33.

3. "L'Europe agricole et l'élargissement du Marché Commun," *Notes et Etudes Documentaires* 4, 061-63 (February 12, 1974): 19; *Le Monde*, November 8, 1963.

4. Hélène Delorme, "Etude de la Représentation des Agriculteurs dans la C.E.E., Rapport provisoire sur l'enquête effectuée en vertu de la Convention no. 18 du 10 mai 1971 entre le Cordes et la F.N.S.P." (Paris: Fondation Nationale des Sciences Politiques, Centre d'Etude des Relations Internationales, n.d.), p. 76.

5. Michael Tracy, *Agriculture in Western Europe* (London: Jonathan Cape, 1964), p. 288.

6. Alfred Grosser, *Germany in Our Time: A Political History of the Postwar Years* (New York: Praeger, 1971), p. 200; *Agra-Europe*, September 30, 1965.

7. Jean Meynaud and Dusan Sidjanski, *Les Groupes de pression dans la communauté européenne*; 1958-1968 (Brussels: Institut d'Etudes Européenes, 1971), p. 196.

8. Yves Malgrain, *L'Intégration agricole dans l'Europe des Six* (Paris: Editions Cujas, 1965), p. 76.

9. Meynaud and Sidjanski, *Les Groupes de pression*, p. 197.

10. Malgrain, *L'Intégration agricole*, p. 142.

11. *Le Monde*, December 3, 1966.

12. Edward Kolodziej, *French International Policy Under de Gaulle and Pompidou* (Ithaca, N.Y.: Cornell University Press, 1974), pp. 263-73; Miriam Camps, *European Unification in the Sixties* (New York: McGraw-Hill, 1966); Roger Morgan, *West European Politics Since 1945: The Shaping of the European Community* (London: Batsford, 1972).

13. Paul Ackermann, *Der Deutsche Bauernverband im politischen Kraftspiel der BRD* (Tübingen: J. C. B. Mohr, 1970), pp. 68 ff.

14. Malgrain, *L'Intégration agricole*, pp. 144-45.

15. F. Roy Willis, *France, Germany and the New Europe* (London: Oxford University Press, 1968), p. 342.

16. Ibid., p. 341.

17. For the operation of the market regulations in the grain sector, see Organization for Economic Cooperation and Development, *Agricultural Policy of the European Economic Community* (Paris: The Organization, 1973), pp. 44-45; Mario Corti, *Politique agricole et construction de l'Europe* (Brussels: Etablissements Emile Bruylant, 1971), pp. 108-11.

18. Malgrain, *L'Intégration agricole*, pp. 145-50.

19. Ackermann, *Der Deutsche Bauernverband*, Chapter 5.

20. *Agra-Europe*, July 22, 1965.

21. Ibid., September 30, 1965.

22. *Le Monde*, December 3, 1966.

23. *Agra-Europe*, December 8, 1966.

24. François-Henri de Virieu, *La Fin d'une agriculture* (Paris: Calmann-Levy, 1967), pp. 35-111; Marcel Faure, Les Paysans dans la société française (Paris: Arman Colin, 1966), pp. 213-14.

25. Willis, *France, Germany and the New Europe*, pp. 287 ff.

26. Yves Tavernier, "Le Syndicalisme paysan et la Cinquième République, 1962-1965," *Revue française de science politique* (October 1966), p. 876.

27. Guy Quaden, *Parité pour l'agriculture et disparité entre agriculteurs* (The Hague: Martins Nijhoff, 1973), p. 211.

28. Jean Deleau, *Le Producteur agricole français* 2 (1974): 5.

29. Henry Roussillon, *L'Association générale des producteurs de blé* (Paris: Fondation Nationale des Sciences Politiques, 1970), pp. 66-70.

30. Ibid., p. 66.

31. *Le Monde*, April 7, 1967.

32. Adrien Zeller, *L'Imbroglio agricole du Marché Commun* (Paris: Calmann-Levy, 1970), p. 56.

33. *Agra-Europe*, January 13, 1966.

34. Ibid., June 8, 1967. The grain market was established by Reglement no. 120/67/CEE of the Council, dated June 13, 1967, *Journal officiel des communautés européennes*, no. 117 (June 19, 1967).

35. *Le Monde*, May 13, 1967.

36. Ibid., June 24, 1967.

37. Deleau, *Le Producteur*, p. 5.

38. See *Agra-Europe*, November 23, 1967, and de Virieu, *La Fin d'une agriculture*, p. 167.

39. *AGPB 1924-1974* (Paris: Editions Erick Grand, 1974), p. 70.

40. LeRoy, *L'Avenir du Marché Commun agricole*, p. 62.

41. Deleau, *Le Producteur*, p. 4.

42. *Le Producteur agricole français* 1 (1974): 13.

43. Joseph LaPalombara, *Politics Within Nations* (Englewood Cliffs, N.J.: Prentice Hall, 1974), Chapter 9.

44. Dusan Sidjanski, interview, Geneva, June 1974.

45. Sicco Mansholt, *La Crise* (Paris: Editions Stock, 1974), pp. 108-115. Mansholt describes the central role of grains and the interests involved, but he does not mention the AGPB in his description of the negotiations leading up to the December 1964 accord.

46. Hélène Delorme, "Le rôle des forces paysannes dans l'élaboration de la politique agricole commune," *Revue française de science politique* 19 (1969): 377.

47. Ibid., p. 378, and interview, October 1974.

48. Glenda Goldstone Rosenthal, *The Man Behind the Decisions: Cases in European Policy-Making* (Lexington, Mass.: Lexington Books, 1975), p. 94.

49. Mansholt, *La Crise*, p. 110.

50. Tavernier, "Le Syndicalisme paysan," p. 887.

51. See Gordon Wright, *Rural Revolution in France* (Stanford, Calif.: Stanford University Press, 1964), pp. 143-82.

52. Jacques and Colette Nême, *Economie européenne* (Paris: Presses Universitaires de France, 1970), p. 212.

53. *Agra-Europe*, November 30, 1967.

54. Ibid., December 7, 1967.

55. Hanns Peter Muth, *French Agriculture and the Political Integration of Western Europe* (Leyden: A. W. Sijthoff, 1970), pp. 241 ff.

56. de Virieu, *La Fin d'une agriculture*, p. 46.

57. Ibid., p. 282; Tavernier, "Le Syndicalisme paysan," pp. 900 ff.

58. Regulation 805/68 of the Council of Ministers; Organization for Economic Cooperation and Development, *Agricultural Policy*, pp. 53-55; "The Common Agricultural Policy Market Organizations and Price Systems," *Newsletter of the Common Agricultural Policy*, 4 (1972): 3-12.

59. *Le Monde*, December 14, 1972; Commission of the European Communities, *Seventh General Report on the Activities of the European Communities* (Brussels, February 1974), p. 271.

60. de Virieu, *La Fin d'une agriculture*, pp. 156-57; see also Faure, *Les Paysans*, p. 277.

61. Organization for Economic Cooperation and Development, *Agricultural Policy in France* (Paris: The Organization, 1974), p. 19.

62. Federal Republic of Germany, Deutscher Bundestag, *Bericht der Bundesregierung über die Lage der Landwirtschaft gemäss 4 Landwirtschaftsgesetz und Massnahmen der Bundesregierung gemäss 5 Landwirtschaftsgesetz und EWG-Anpassungsgesetz* (Bonn, 1970), p. 204.

63. Willis, *France, Germany and the New Europe*, p. 338.

64. Commission of the European Communities, *Second General Report on the Activities of the European Communities* (Brussels, February 1968), pp. 154-55.

65. Hélène Delorme and Yves Tavernier, *Les Paysans français et l'Europe* (Paris: Fondation Nationale des Sciences Politiques, 1969), p. 92.

66. Organization for Economic Cooperation and Development, *Agricultural Policy*, pp. 56-57.

67. Delorme and Tavernier, *Les Paysans français*, pp. 94-99.

68. *Agra-Europe*, December 16, 1965.

69. Roger Morgan, *West European Politics Since 1945: The Shaping of the European Community* (London: Batsford, 1972), pp. 182-83.

70. Interview, January 1975.

71. *Agra-Europe*, January 20, 1965.

72. Ibid., December 16, 1965.

73. Theodor Heidhues, "Voraussetzungen und Möglichkeiten einer Neuorientierung in der Agrarpolotik," *Agrarwirtschaft* 33 (1969): 13.

74. Ibid.

75. Economic Development Committee for Agriculture, *U.K. Farming and the Common Market: Milk and Milk Products* (London: National Economic Development Office, March 1973), pp. 38-39.

76. *Agra-Europe*, March 10, 1966.

77. Ibid., March 3 and 10, 1966; *Frankfürter Allgemeine Zeitung*, March 3 and 5, 1966.

78. *Agra-Europe*, March 31, 1966.

79. Ibid., June 9, 1966; *Common Market* 6 (1966): 142.

80. Wolfram F. Hanrieder, *The Stable Crisis: Two Decades of German Foreign Policy* (New York; Harper & Row, 1970), p. 68.

81. *Agra-Europe*, May 19, 1966.

82. Ibid.

83. Ibid., June 16, 1966.

84. Interview, January 1975.

85. Georges Estievenart, *Les Partis politiques en Allemagne fédérale* (Paris: Presses Universitaires de France, 1973), p. 118.

86. Ibid.

87. Andreas Leitholf, *Das Einwirken der Wirtschaftsverbände auf die Agrarmarktorganization der EWG* (Baden-Baden: Nomos Verlagsgesellschaft, 1971).

88. Grosser, *Germany*, p. 187.

89. Estievenart, *Les Partis politiques*, p. 54.

90. *Agra-Europe*, January 18, 1968.

91. Delorme and Tavernier, *Les paysans français*, p. 97.

92. *Agra-Europe*, October 26, 1967.

93. Malgrain, *L'Intégration agricole*, p. 54.

94. Delorme and Tavernier, *Les paysans français*, pp. 92-94.

95. Ibid., pp. 94-99.

5

COPA AND EC
POLICY MAKING
IN AGRICULTURE

Up to this point, we have looked at the activities of national farm groups in France and Germany when they were confronted with Community regulations in areas where previously only national regulations had prevailed. The reactions of the interest groups varied, but in general the EC needed to offer extremely attractive benefits, as well as safeguarding any particularly valuable national links that the interest groups wanted to preserve—for example, the AGPB and the stocking boards (*organismes stockeurs*)—before these groups shifted their allegiance to the new EC arrangement.

Another aspect of the impact of the EC on national interest-group strategies concerns these groups' efforts to act on the Community level through Community interest groups. I have used the term "Eurogroup" to designate these new interest groups, which operate on the Community level in order to influence Community decisions.

In this chapter we shall look at an important Eurogroup in detail. We shall study the institutionalization of COPA and the place of COPA in the EC's policy-making process.

Eurogroups are to be found in practically all areas in which the EC has acted. They arose in three waves in reaction to the three great movements toward developing European institutions after World War II: the first came with the creation of the Organization for European Economic Cooperation, the second with the European Coal and Steel Community (ECSC), and the third with the European Economic Community.[1] This third wave was the most substantial, from the standpoint of both the number and the strength of the Eurogroups that it involved.

In terms of the resources devoted to agriculture by the Community, the time and energy of EC and national officials concerned with it, and the significance of the crises associated with it, the agricultural sector may be considered to be the prime sector of Community activity. Hence it is not surprising that COPA, the major farm Eurogroup, is one of the oldest and most active of the professional organizations established on the Community level. COPA's potential as an interest group capable of commanding the assent of its constituent member organizations, as well as the respect of its interlocutors in the EC institutions, will be assessed. To the extent that COPA is a viable organization capable of outlining a course of action and then successfully persuading its members to adhere to it, one may argue that the transfer of decision making in farm policy from national spheres to the Community sphere has fundamentally altered the way in which national interest groups seek to influence these decisions. Instead of continuing to rely mainly on national channels to influence Community decisions, these national groups will have acknowledged the necessity of surrendering some of their own autonomy to the Eurogroup in order to gain access to EC institutions.

On the other hand, to the extent that COPA seems to have basic limitations built into its organization that reduce it to a coordinating body and a place for information exchange, one is justified in maintaining that national groups and national patterns of access to decision makers preserve most of their vitality.

This chapter looks at COPA as an organization existing in a certain environment, facing certain resource constraints, obliged to define its actions in light of certain givens in the form of the EC institutions with which it has to deal. The chapter attempts to answer four questions: How important is COPA? What are the limits to its growth? Is COPA taking over functions that previously were performed exclusively by national farm groups? Is COPA placing constraints on the behavior of these national groups that did not exist before the EC?

Before considering COPA as a functioning organization, we should reemphasize the nature of the Community's decision-making system. In general, it is the Commission that proposes measures and the Council of Ministers that takes the final decisions, which are binding on member states and their citizens. At several points along the way, certain bodies such as the European Parliament and the Economic and Social Council have the right to advise the Commission and the Council (the latter always has the final word, however). In addition, a multitude of advisory bodies (the Special Committee on Agriculture, the management committees, the consultative committees, and the Committee of Permanent Representatives) are used by the Council and the Commission to prepare the dossiers under consideration.

The Commission, charged by the Rome Treaty with the task of submitting proposals to the Council, has a general policy of declining official, public contact with national interest groups. Hence the potential importance of COPA is clear:

To the extent that the Commission shuts itself off from contact with national economic- and social-group spokesmen, these same national groups are obliged to use a Eurogroup to influence the first stage of decision making, in which the proposals are formulated by the Commission.[2]

Of course, to the extent that the Commission makes direct contact with national groups, the above "official" version of relationships between the Community and interest groups loses its validity. This chapter is an attempt to reveal to what extent, if any, this has in fact occurred.

ORIGINS OF COPA

COPA was founded during the first year of the Community's existence. At the Stresa Conference in July 1958, the Commission, anxious to make contact with farm leaders, discussed the formation of official links with the farm delegations from the six member states. On September 6, 1958, the main farm organizations of the Six founded the Comité Professionnel des Organisations Agricoles de la CEE. This body was reorganized and named the Comité des Organisations Professionnelles Agricoles on April 3, 1959.[3]

The founding organizations of COPA[4] were:

Germany:	Deutscher Bauernverband: the only national farmers' union in Germany at that time; highly centralized
Belgium:	Alliance Agricole Belge: Walloon Catholic but open to non-Catholics
	Belgisches Boerenbond: Flemish Catholic
	Fédération Nationale des Unions Professionnelles Agricoles: neutral religiously and ideologically
	These were the three major Belgian farm groups.
France:	Assemblée Permanente des Chambres d'Agriculture: a semi-official organization, elected by all farmers, supported by a government land tax
	Confederation Nationale de la Mutualité, de la Coopération et du Credit Agricoles: the cooperative movement
	Fédération Nationale des Syndicats d'Exploitants Agricoles: the national farmers' interest group, including member organizations specialized by product as well as member federations for each *département*
Italy:	Confederazione Nazionale dei Coltivatori Doretti: mainly Christian Democratic organization representing small farmers
	Confederazione Generale dell'Agricoltura Italiana: farm owners' organization
	Federazione Italiana dei Consorzi Agrari: left-leaning organization controlling consortia or distribution of fertilizers, seeds, etc., created by agrarian reform

Luxembourg: Centrale Paysanne Luxembourgeoise
Netherlands: Katholieke Nederlandse Boeren- en Tuindersbond
Koninklijk Nederlands Landbouwcomite
Nederlandse Christelijke Boren- en Tuindersbond

The organizations that founded COPA were, at the time, the major farm groups of the Six; COPA could therefore claim to be the single Eurogroup that represented all farmers in the Six. By the end of the 1960s, however, the major national farm organizations had been challenged by rival groups in countries such as France and Italy, and even in Germany the DBV was threatened by dissident groups, some of which were to secede in the early 1970s. This splintering process affecting the national interest groups, together with its effect on COPA, will be discussed later in this chapter. COPA's membership was increased in 1967, when it was joined by the CNJA, the young farmers' group in France. COPA was expanded further in 1973 when Denmark, Ireland, and the United Kingdom joined the Community. With the enlargement of the EC, seven new national organizations joined COPA.[5]

Denmark: De samvirkende danske Landbo-foreninger
Landbrugsraadet
De samvirkende danske Husmands-foreninger
Ireland: Irish Farmers' Association
United Kingdom: National Farmers' Union of England and Wales
National Farmers' Union of Scotland
Ulster Farmers' Union

COPA's membership has remained unchanged since 1973.

COPA is a "peak association." Its membership, strictly speaking, consists of other organizations, all of which are organized within national systems. COPA's decisions are therefore filtered through the headquarters of the national farm groups, which apply them as they wish—or refuse to apply them, as they wish. For example, a French farmer is a member of his departmental federation and the FNSEA; he is not a member of COPA. Most national farm groups themselves are peak associations, in fact. This is true of the DBV, the CNJA, the FNSEA, and others. These organizations already embody a kind of interest-group federalism; so the leadership in Bonn or Paris rests on geographical and function sub-groups. COPA is one more layer added onto these organizations.

It is clear, then, that the national and European farm organizations are aggregating interests at the same time as they are articulating them. One of the errors of structural-functional analyses when first used in political science was the assumption that interest groups mainly articulated interests. Looking at the operation of COPA, one sees that this is not so: From the time that German farmers discuss policy in their *Land* organization and French farmers do so in their *département* group, the process of aggregation begins. It continues as one goes up the organizational ladder to the national federations in Paris and Bonn and then to COPA, with compromises occurring at each step to a higher level.

Another aspect of this creation of an additional organizational level imposed upon the older national interest-group systems is that the individual farmer is even more removed from the Eurogroup leaders than he is from the leaders of his national association.

The elites that have the greatest resources to dominate national farm groups are also the ones that dominate COPA. The skills needed to work through COPA in order to influence EC policy accentuate the diversity of political resources among various groups of farmers. National farm policy in France or Germany is complex enough, but EC farm policy is so Byzantine that only farmers with large amounts of resources, especially time, knowledge, and wealth, are able to understand the decision-making process sufficiently to be able to influence the output.

COPA leaders thus represent an elite of elites. They are drawn from large-scale agriculture, chiefly in product areas such as grains and highly capitalized livestock operations. Most of the members of the COPA Presidium own more than 100 hectares of land.[6] (The average Community farm is only 17 hectares.)[7] This aspect of COPA was one of the causes of the creation of an anti-COPA, anti-EC farmers' group in the late 1960s, which chose to organize on the Community level in order to fight the objectionable policies of the Community.

After two years of largely ad hoc operations, COPA in 1960 endowed itself with the standard array of institutions: Assembly, executive board, president, and Secretariat.[8] The Assembly does not develop policy itself; it is a legitimizing institution.

The executive board, or Presidium, is composed of "one permanent representative for each member organisation." Each representative is a leader of the national farm group. Countries such as Germany that have only one member organization may send an additional representative (this does not change the number of votes possessed by that organization). The president summons the Presidium, usually once a month.

All policy stands are discussed in the Presidium, including positions on Commission and Council actions, planning for farm demonstrations, and coordination of lobbying at the national level. Officials of the Commission often meet with the Presidium to discuss EC farm policy, especially the price proposals of the Commission for the coming harvest year. Commission officials most frequently attending Presidium meetings include the commissioner, the director-general and the assistant directors-general, and the division head of the office in charge of relations with nongovernmental organizations. The Presidium is the highest decision-making body of COPA and has access to the highest levels of the Commission.

The president of COPA speaks in the name of the organization, convenes the Presidium, and presides over the Assembly. The president is elected by the Presidium from among its members for a two-year term. The 1973 reorganization of COPA significantly strengthened the leadership potential of the president; this reorganization will be examined below.

In addition to the Assembly, Presidium, and president, COPA has a permanent Secretariat composed of a secretary-general and an administrative staff.

COPA is almost as old as the EC itself. COPA has changed together with the institutions and policies of the EC, especially, of course, those concerned with farm policy. COPA has become a more complex, differentiated organization in the past two decades in order to deal with a more challenging institutional environment.

INSTITUTIONALIZATION OF COPA

In assessing the institutionalization of COPA we need to consider several aspects of its development: organizational resources (men and money), the development of its institutions, and changes in its decision rules (unanimity or majority voting), and its links with its environment (the EC institutions, on the one hand, and its component national organizations, on the other).

Organizational Resources

The organizational resources of COPA come entirely from the national interest groups that compose it. Unlike some national interest groups that receive government subsidies (such as the officially recognized French groups), COPA receives no subsidies from the Community institutions. The contributions of member organizations are based on the percentage allotted to each member state: 25 percent each for Germany, France, and Italy, and 25 percent for Benelux, before 1973.[9] After 1973, this ratio was changed to: 4/23 each for Germany, France, Italy, and the United Kingdom; 2/23 each for Belgium, the Netherlands, and Denmark; 1/23 for Ireland; and a lump sum for Luxembourg.[10]

COPA's budget has grown appreciably: In the first year of operation, 1959, its budget was approximately $17,500, barely enough to support a single staff member and his operations. By 1975, the budget had grown to more than $600,000. Figure 7 displays the growth of the COPA budget.

As can be seen, the enlargement of COPA resulting from the entry of the seven new farm groups from Denmark, Ireland, and the United Kingdom was accompanied by a leap in budgetary funds. The main force behind this increase was the insistence of the National Farmers' Union (NFU) in the United Kingdom, together with the Scottish and Ulster unions, that COPA be strengthened

FIGURE 7

COPA Budget, 1959-75

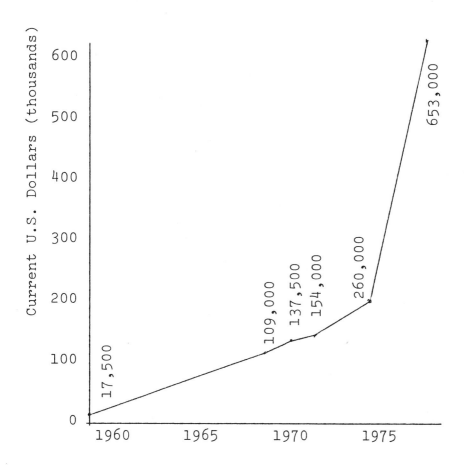

Sources: Turuel T. Nielsen, "Notes on Interest Aggregation and Articulation in the European Community: C.O.P.A.," in *Symposium Europa: 1950-1970* (Bruges, Belgium: College of Europe, 1971); interviews, December 1974-March 1975; COPA documents.

in order to work even more closely with EC institutions. The NFU, accustomed to a quasi-corporatist relationship with the British Government and reputed to be one of the most effective professional groups in the United Kingdom, is determined to increase the resources of COPA in the future, according to informed observers.[11]

At the same time, the NFU strives to maintain the United Kingdom Price Review, during which it confers with the Minister of Agriculture on farm prices for the coming year (most of which, of course, are now decided in the Council of the EC).[12] The NFU is an example of a national farm group that initially feared the entry of British agriculture into the common agricultural policy. Nevertheless, having been thrust into the EC by the action of its government, the NFU now seeks to strengthen COPA's participation in EC price negotiations.

With the increase in its budget, COPA has been able to increase its staff accordingly. The Secretariat grew from two people in 1959 (of whom one had academic training) to thirty-five in 1975 (of whom thirteen had academic training, not counting eight translators).[13]

Institutional Development

COPA's institutional development has responded to the growth of the Community's agricultural policy. As the common agricultural policy expanded, COPA's structure evolved to permit it to follow the complexities of Community farm policy. Around 1966, the COPA Secretariat first set up a division of labor among its experts so that they could specialize in certain topics.[14] The Secretariat is now divided into three divisions: General and Economic Affairs (in charge of the annual price review, economic and statistical questions), Animal Products (milk and milk products, beef, pork, and so on), and Vegetable Specialized Products (grains, rice, fruit, vegetables, and so on).[15] In 1971, the COPA Presidium named a special committee to study possible reorganization in order to cope with the entry of British, Danish, and Irish farm associations. The British and the Danish farmers were especially sophisticated in dealing with their own governments, and COPA wanted to take advantage of their skills, especially in order to advance certain claims, such as the establishment of an annual price review for the Community similar to the practice in Great Britain.

On April 5, 1973, the COPA Presidium finally adopted major changes in the organization.[16] The General Assembly now became a congress, which would meet once a year. The Presidium received one permanent member from each of the national organizations, chosen from among their leaders. The voting would now be done according to qualified majority, with each country having a certain number of votes. According to the new rules:

The votes of all representatives of a country's organization will be weighted as follows:

Belgium: 6
Denmark: 6
Germany: 12
France: 12

Ireland: 4
Italy: 12
Luxembourg: 2
The Netherlands: 6
United Kingdom: 12

The qualified majority is 52 votes.[17]

In practice, however, qualified majority voting is used only on budgetary questions, not on major policy matters.[18] Additional important changes were the election of the president by the Presidium and the expansion of his term to two years. This would permit the president to master the complexities of EC policies and improve the continuity of COPA's policy stands.

Links with Decision-Making Environment

The major elements in the decision-making environment with which COPA keeps in contact are the two main organs of the EC, on the one hand (the Commission and the Council), and the national member organizations on the other.

From the beginning, COPA had close contacts with the Directorate-General for Agriculture in the Commission. The commissioner for agriculture, Mansholt, drew up the ground rules for Commission-COPA contacts in January 1959. These rules gave the initiative to the Commission in the relationship.[19] When it is recalled that COPA was formed in large part because of Mansholt's initiative in the first place, it is clear that at that time COPA was mainly a device by which the Commission could communicate to the farmers and give itself legitimacy by showing to the public that it was consulting with "Community" farm representatives.

In the following years, COPA worked for a closer consultative relationship with the Commission. COPA has succeeded in obtaining more regularly scheduled meetings with representatives of the Agriculture Directorate-General of the Commission. But COPA still objects to such things as the leaking of documents by Commission staff members to newsmen or national farm organizations before COPA has had a chance to see them. This becomes an especially thorny problem if, for example, a French staff member of the Commission leaks working papers to the leaders of a French farm group: COPA's leadership is at a disadvantage in working for a compromise position among its member organizations when one of them possesses this kind of inside information on the Commission's intentions.

In general, COPA staff members have frequent access to middle-level Commission officials, especially with middle-level officials, while the political leadership of COPA has frequent contact at the Commissioner level. In the table below we see the major links between the Commission and COPA. In addition, informal contacts link the two.

COPA contacts with the Council of Ministers have been sporadic and difficult to establish. The reason, of course, is that the Council represents the national governments and prefers to remain aloof from contact with Eurogroups or national interest groups, at least in theory. In practice, Council sessions are held amid throngs of journalists and other observers, and lobbying by interest-

TABLE 1

Links between COPA and the EC Commission

COPA	Commission
Presidium of COPA (highest political level)	Agricultural commissioner—monthly meetings; president of the Commission—meetings on exceptional occasions
Staff of COPA (Secretariat)	Direction G of D.G. VI, unit "relations avec les organisations non gouvernementales," and other directions of DG VI.
COPA experts	Direction G liaison unit above, as well as *chefs de division* for specific products—informal, confidential meetings on current problems
COPA experts (tied to the national member groups, e.g., the delegates of the French wheat producers' group, AGPB)	Consultative Committee attended by *chef de division* for product concerned, e.g., Direction B-1, "cereals and derived products"

group representatives is not infrequent. At least one farm lobbyist (reputedly of the Italian Coltivatori Diretti) sits in on Council meetings from time to time.[20] Defending a proposal to open Council meetings to the public, E. Gazzo, editor of *Agence Europe*, declared:

> It's preposterous to argue that Council meetings should not be thrown open to the public since that would destroy the secrecy which is necessary to arrive at compromises. The Council meetings, in effect, are not secret for the newspapermen or for interest group spokesmen who practically stand behind the ministers during the meetings.[21]

Interest-group contact does take place, therefore, but in a disjointed and informal way.

National interest groups have made public approaches to the Council several times; for example, the Breton farm leaders have made several direct approaches. As for COPA, it has had less success in establishing regular contacts with the Council. By the mid-1960s, the COPA Presidium was sending telegrams to the Council before all important sessions on farm policy, recalling COPA's position and demanding favorable action for Europe's farmers. And COPA requested regular, informal contacts with the Council of Ministers.[22]

Since 1970, COPA has in fact obtained the right to have informal meetings with the president of the Council of Ministers.[23] Some of these meetings were publicly announced. For example, the COPA Presidium on January 13, 1971, decided to request a meeting with the president of the Council, Michel Cointat of France. Two weeks later, Cointat met the Presidium, but he received it in his capacity as Minister of Agriculture for France, not as president of the Council of Ministers.[24] An interesting example of COPA–Council contacts occurred in the fall of 1974. The Presidium met Christian Bonnet, the French Minister of Agriculture who was then president of the Council, on September 4, 1974. Their purpose, in the words of one Presidium member, was to reaffirm "their unanimity and their solidarity. This is important, because certain ministers are saying the opposite."[25] This meeting occurred shortly before the Council was to rule on the Commission's proposal for emergency supplementary aid to Community farmers. COPA was attempting to present a unified front to the Council through Bonnet, because Ertl, the German Minister of Agriculture, had been arguing that the Community farmers were not in fact united on the subject of a price rise, because he knew that the DBV was not thoroughly behind such a stand. The COPA meeting (which, in turn, had been motivated by the French FNSEA) had as its goal counteracting this view, which was being defended inside the Council.[26] (The details of this maneuver by the FNSEA to use COPA in order to bolster the French position inside the Council against the Germans will be examined in Chapter 7.)

COPA has succeeded, therefore, in maintaining contacts with the Council for the past four or five years, but these contacts remain informal and unstructured. Much of the effectiveness of these contacts depends in fact on the relationship between the national minister who happens to be president of the Council and his own national farm groups at the time of the request for a meeting.

The Committee of Permanent Representatives (CPR), which is a permanent screening body for the Council, seems to have prevented direct contact with COPA. The members of the CPR, because it is, in effect, a group of country missions attached to the EC, naturally get their information and instructions from their national governments. The agricultural counselor of a major member state's permanent representative has stated:

I never come into contact with COPA. Officially, all my instructions
come from the Foreign Ministry; unofficially, often the Agriculture
Ministry talks to me directly without channelling their views through
the Foreign Ministry. As far as interest groups go, sometimes I talk
to [the Brussels representatives of a national farm group] .[27]

Neither the French nor the German agricultural counselor of the Committee of
Permanent Representatives maintains personal contacts with COPA.[28] If members of the Committee of Permanent Representatives want to talk to interest
groups, they talk to their own national groups and not to COPA.

COPA has close ties with the European Parliament, but COPA leaders admit the powerlessness of the Parliament. It is used mainly because it is there and
the costs of using it are low.

PROBLEMS OF COPA

COPA's weaknesses relate to access to the Commission, the creation of
potentially competitive Eurogroups, and competition from purely national interest groups. As can be seen, all of these problems stem essentially from COPA's
difficulties in maintaining its position as the sole spokesmen for Community
farmers. To the extent that this position is eroded (from the inside by the
preference of the Commission for direct contacts with national groups or from
the outside by competitor groups) COPA's basic function is threatened.

Access to the Commission

Because of the institutional structure of the EC, the relationship with the
Commission remains COPA's primary *raison d'être*. It was the Commission,
specifically the Agriculture Directorate-General under Mansholt, that was
largely responsible for the foundation of COPA in the first place. The reasoning
of the Commission was that it could perhaps rearrange the traditional political
patterns of the member states by insisting that national interest groups approach
the Commission through the newly formed Eurogroups. COPA's main role, then,
was to serve as spokesman for the national farm interest groups of the Community. And because the Council was more amenable to national channels of
access leading through each minister, the Commission remained COPA's major
interlocutor among EC institutions. Furthermore, the Commission's task of
formulating the proposals on which the Council would eventually rule made
this relationship extremely important for COPA.

Obviously, COPA's role as major Community farm spokesman is endangered every time the Commission engages in direct contacts with national farm

groups, bypassing COPA. In theory, the Commission never does this.[29] But if we look beyond and behind the official theory of how Community institutions work, we shall find that the Commission does in fact consult national groups directly from time to time.

A notable resort by Mansholt to direct contacts with national farm organizations occurred in 1969 and 1970, when he was publicizing his memorandum for structural reform, known as the Mansholt Plan. This plan was designed to solve the problem the Community had been facing in agriculture: The sizable expenditure by the EC support fund was threatening the Community budget; yet it did not seem to be helping most farmers at all. Their incomes continued to fall, leading to severe unrest in the countryside. Mansholt advocated a Community program of improvement for farms over a certain size, special aid to small farmers and old farmers to leave agriculture, and restraint of price increases in order to reduce EC expenditures in the long run.[30]

As part of his "lobbying in reverse," Mansholt visited several EC states. He realized that his actions were endangering COPA's function. At the Paris meeting in October 1970, he stated that he did not want to "short-circuit" COPA but that he wanted to know the positions of each national farm organization before these positions were changed through COPA's compromises.[31]

Mansholt had taken over COPA's function of examining the positions of the national organizations. Instead of permitting COPA to reach a compromise and present a united stand on the Mansholt Plan to the Commission, Mansholt decided to aggregate the stands of the national farm groups himself and then advise the Council accordingly. For example, on November 30-December 1, 1970, a secret meeting of the Council was held on the difficult agricultural situation in the Community. Mansholt told the farm ministers of his recent contacts with the national farm organizations and argued strongly for the need to enact a program of structural reform in order to solve the farm crisis.[32]

The Commission, and especially the agriculture commissioner, often finds itself facing contradictory goals with respect to Eurogroups, and this case of Mansholt and his lobbying for the Mansholt Plan in 1970 illustrates the dilemma well. The Commission must choose either to let the Eurogroup speak for the national groups, and hence trust the Eurogroup's interest aggregation, or else it must choose to go to the national groups itself. Both courses of action have advantages and disadvantages. The first bolsters the standing of the Eurogroup, and all the things connected with this: fostering the growth of Community-level political activities, altering the national political patterns, and so on. But it means that the Commission does not know the views of the national groups firsthand. The second course of action provides the Commission with direct knowledge of the national groups' positions, but it undercuts the position of COPA.

Unfortunately for the Eurogroup's fate, the evidence shows that the higher the stakes and the bigger the issue, the more inclined a commissioner will be to make his own contacts with national groups, to find out for himself what is going on at the national level, instead of trusting the Eurogroup to do this for him. The conclusion is that Eurogroups will be used by the Commission more often for secondary issues and problems.

There is an additional, more fundamental factor at work that has been favoring direct contacts between the Commission and national groups in the past five years. It stems from the "nationalization" of the Commission, which began in the mid-1960s and has continued to the present. Commissioners and their staffs are increasingly conscious of their separate national identities and loyalties, and consequently they give only lip service to the official picture of the Commission, treating only with groups organized on the European level.

This nationalization of the Commission occurred against a backdrop of wider and deeper changes in the nature of the Community, including the weakening of prospects for the Commission as a strong supranational institution. In a very real sense, the fate of the Commission is the fate of the Community as a supranational, as opposed to a confederal, organization. With the decline of the prospects for a strong Commission went the increased role of more conventional bodies such as the Committee of Permanent Representatives, in which the supranational search for the "European interest" gave way to traditional diplomatic bargaining. A thorough explanation of why this is so would be in large part the story of the Community itself. A few of the major reasons for the circumscription of the Commission deserve to be presented, however.

From the beginning, institutional constraints on the Commission were imposing enough to give the most optimistic supranationalist pause. The Rome Treaty lodges the final power of decision in the Council, whose concerns are inevitably national; even if the Commission pursues European goals, it must contend with the dominant national interests of member states in order for its proposals to have a possibility of passing the Council and becoming Community law. The development of the Community up to the mid-1960s in such fields as trade liberalization and agriculture resulted in large part from a Franco-German Commission triangle, where Germany sought increased trade and legitimacy, France sought financial aid for its agriculture and a European base for its ambitious diplomacy, and the Commission sought the construction of Community policies. When this fabric of interests began to become unraveled in the second half of the 1960s, supranational initiatives collapsed. The constitutional crisis of 1965 was a watershed in the development of the Community because its resolution in the form of the 1966 Luxembourg Accords entailed abandonment of majority voting within the Council (that had been called for in the Rome Treaty), imposition of restrictions on the exercise of Community initiatives in the development and publicizing of its policy proposals, and strengthening of the role of the Council's Committee of Permanent Representatives as a confederal counterweight to the Commission.[33]

There is an inherent tension between the Commission's bureaucratic character and the political role it was expected to play: "The Commission's main function in the Community decision making process is to provide political impetus and leadership towards European goals. Yet the Commission's formal powers are not those normally associated with political leadership."[34] The Commission was a hybrid institution, much more so than its predecessor, the High Authority of the European Coal and Steel Community (ECSC).[35]

This ambiguity in the Commission's role and the unmistakable power residing in the Council meant that the Commission soon felt the effects of changes in Community politics. As the economic and monetary conditions of Community states worsened in the late 1960s, the impetus to construct common policies for the EC weakened. Exchange-rate disturbances threatened to destroy the common agricultural policy as compensatory levies arose around states that revalued or devalued their currencies. The enlargement of the Community proved to be a mixed blessing, increasing the heterogeneity of the members and subjecting Community policies to extensive reexaminations by the British. The resolution of Germany's eastern questions effectively removed the stigma of World War II, and both Willy Brandt and Helmut Schmidt strongly asserted the legitimacy of German interests in the Community. The war in the 1973 Middle East provided the EC with an opportunity to take united action in the diplomatic and energy fields. Conflicting national interests (as well as intense U.S. pressure) prevented Community initiatives in the Middle East and in relations with oil producers.[36]

A renewed, acute awareness of national objectives has dominated Community politics for the past few years. National objectives were pursued, to be sure, before 1965; the difference is that, formerly, they were pursued in a Community context and their pursuit resulted in Community policies, which is not the case today.

As member states have reemphasized their national goals to the detriment of Community endeavors, so has the Commission lost ground to the Council and its subsidiary institutions. The Committee of Permanent Representatives, basically a committee of member states' ambassadors to the EC, gained increased importance after 1965, and intergovernmental committees have proliferated alongside the Committee of Permanent Representatives.[37]

The nationalization of the Commission, due basically to the ambiguity in the Commission's role and important diplomatic developments in the member states, was reinforced by changes in Commission elites from 1960 to 1975. By the end of the 1960s, the "old guard" of the original commissioners had practically disappeared. Only Mansholt stayed on until 1972. With the first generation of commissioners went the original idealism of the European enterprise. The second-generation elite had a much more pragmatic, specific conception of their office. As one Commission official put it:

After 1969, a nibbling away (*grignotage*) of the Commission began. The new commissioners were more "national," and they lacked the European spirit of the original ones. So now, for example, it's not unusual at all to see Soames talk to English groups or Spinelli talk to Italian ones. And the other commissioners will now not hesitate to talk to interest groups that are not in their own field. For example, Soames and Spinelli will talk to English or Italian farmers, even though it's Lardinois's job to take care of them. This was unheard of before 1969.[38]

Elite changes reinforced the broader transformations of the Community's institutions.

The Commission's informal quota system for top offices (division chiefs and above) has also reinforced the broader nationalizing trends. The quota system became more important after the fusion of the three communities into one in 1967. In the next few years, the new Commission formed from the union of three former executives had to reduce slowly its personnel in order to eliminate duplication by the former ECSC, Euratom, and EEC officials. This was carried out according to a quota system, and those officials who had to be shuffled around were induced to acquiesce by techniques such as the "golden handshake," by which a considerable salary increase was the compensation for transfer to a less important post.[39]

This long-term nationalization of the Commission will greatly affect its relations with COPA. As the Commission itself approaches national groups directly, the responsibility of COPA to represent these national groups is undermined. When the nationalization of the Commission is added to the specific advantages for a commissioner to go directly to national groups instead of using COPA (as was discussed with regard to Mansholt in 1970), it is clear that COPA is encountering great difficulties in strengthening its role from the Commission itself.

Competitive Eurogroups

COPA is threatened not only if its main interlocuter, the Commission, prefers to go to national groups, but also if certain national groups decide to form different Eurogroups. Thus, instead of being the sole representative body on the Community level for farmers, as it was in the early 1960s, COPA would be one of several such organizations. If this occurred, its situation would resemble that of the FNSEA in France, which is faced with competitors on the left (MODEF), on the right (the FFA), and sometimes from within (big farmers of the AGPB, reformists of the CNJA).

There have been attempts to form Eurogroups outside of COPA. One early, abortive attempt was the consideration by the AGPB of France to found a European wheat producers' organization. The sugar beet producers already had a separate European organization, Confederation Interprofessionnel des Betteraviers Européens (CIBE), which then developed an EC division. So the leaders of the AGPB seriously considered a Eurogroup for wheat and other grains. But their idea met the opposition of farmers in countries such as Germany in which the specialized associations such as wheat producers are closely linked to the national farmers' group. A separate European group for these specialized associations would threaten the unity of the general national farm federation. The Commission also dissuaded Deleau: It did not want to see COPA's unity endangered.[40] So the AGPB project never materialized.

Another instance of a separate Eurogroup was the foundation of a family farmers' organization in 1970. The impetus for this organization came from MODEF, the Communist-supported family farm group of France. In early 1970 MODEF, the National Alliance of Italian Farmers, the National Association of Italian Agricultural Cooperatives, the Sharecroppers' Federation, and the Action Committee of Walloon Peasants founded the Commission of Permanent Cooperation. The new group attacked the "monopoly" of COPA and said that the Mansholt Plan threatened the future of family farming in the EC.[41] In July 1972, the group changed its name to the *Comité Européen pour le Progrès Agricole* (European Committee for Agricultural Progress, COMEPRA). It asked that the Commission recognize it as a valid spokesman, like COPA; it condemned the common agricultural policy for giving excessive profits to "big capitalists." (On the other hand, COMEPRA at the same time condemned the United States for its attacks on the EC.)[42] By late 1972, COMEPRA's membership had expanded to include other small farm groups in the member states such as the Democratic Farmers' Action of Germany, the National League of Family Farmers of Ireland, and the Peasant Party of the Netherlands.[43]

COMEPRA has succeeded to some extent in obtaining recognition from the Commission, even though the group is considered by many Commission officials to be merely a "troublemaker." The Commission argues that COMEPRA is composed mainly of farmers in two member states, France and Italy, and that its Communist connections make it more of a blatantly political instrument than a spokesman for farm interests. Nevertheless, because the Commission had recognized Communist unions as being representative spokesmen for French and Italian farm workers in April 1969 and permitted them to participate on the agricultural consultative committees, it was difficult for the Commission to deny COMEPRA's request for recognition in 1972.[44]

The Commission has always tried to help the formation of Eurogroups, in order to secure support for Community initiatives and rearrange the patterns of domestic politics in member states, but why has it opposed the formation of agricultural Eurogroups such as the unsuccessful project for a wheat producers' organization and the more successful COMEPRA? The answer concerns, in part, the Commission's desire to maintain the unity of COPA as the sole representative of farmers in the Community. A chief reason for the Commission's support of COPA has been the convenience of dealing with a single organization that could aggregate the demands of the national farm organizations and present the Commission with a single set of demands in the name of all European farmers. The proliferation of Eurogroups would make the Commission's work more difficult.

In addition, not all Eurogroups will support the Commission or the Community itself. In the case of COMEPRA, several national farm groups organized on the EC level in order to denounce the whole Community enterprise. Such groups produce considerable embarrassment for the Commission. Not only do they show that all is not for the best in the sectors administered by the Community, such as agriculture. It is also dangerous for the Commission to deal openly with these groups if they represent political forces opposed to the current governments of key member states. In the case of COMEPRA, the Commission was asked to confer legitimacy on a Eurogroup, the most important members of which were Italian and French farmers of Communist leanings, at a time when the left in both countries was developing a serious bid for power. In Italy, the Communists' gains led to discussions of a "historic compromise" under which the Christian Democrats would admit them to a governing coalition. In France the left was recovering from its losses after the 1968 upheaval, and its unity permitted Mitterand to come within one percentage point of winning the presidency in 1974. Given such internal political conditions in key member states, how could the Commission run the risk of increasing the prestige of Communist interest groups on the Community level? And in view of the increasing nationalization of the Commission in the 1970s, surely there were implicit or explicit orders from the national governments concerned that Commission officials exercise discretion in dealings with groups such as COMEPRA.

These competitive Eurogroups do not help COPA, of course. They threaten the claims of unanimity, unity, and legitimacy that COPA can make; as one Commission official explained:

> When COPA began in 1958, it could claim, correctly, that it represented *all* the farm organizations of the Community, with the exception of some tiny fringes. Since then, the situation has changed, and dissident groups have arisen, such as COMEPRA, which challenge this claim.[45]

The existence of rival groups, then, is a second difficulty that COPA must resolve if it wishes to strengthen its position on the Community level.

EC-Level Activities Undertaken by National Groups

COPA's role as farm spokesman on the EC level is threatened not only when the Commission goes directly to national groups or by the formation of competing EC-level groups. It is also threatened when national groups decide to undertake activities on the EC level. Some of these activities will be examined in Chapter 6, which includes attempts to find out when and why they decide to use other means of influencing Community farm decisions. Therefore, merely a brief description of this kind of activity will be given here.

It is highly significant that almost all of the EC-level activities organized by national groups have resulted from the initiatives of French groups, specifically, the FNSEA. An important exception was the massive demonstration that occurred before the Council of Ministers in March 1971, in which 150,000-200,000 farmers took part, resulting in the death of one farmer and the wounding of scores of policemen and demonstrators. This demonstration was organized by the Front Vert (Green Front), grouping three of the main Belgian farm organizations. The major grievances of the farmers concerned the smallness of the price increases recommended by the Commission after a price freeze for the three previous years, as well as the proposals for structural reform put forward by Mansholt, which many farmers considered to be the destruction of the family farm. At the last minute, other COPA members joined the demonstration, principally French farmers. The General Assembly of COPA was held at Brussels on March 25, the day of the demonstration and of the Council of Ministers session.[46]

The Belgian farm organizations were strategically placed for such a demonstration because of the ease of transporting the farmers to Brussels. COPA itself did not initiate the plans for the demonstration: As one Commission official observed, "COPA was not really behind the demonstration; it was other forces entirely."[47] The role of the COPA Assembly the morning of the demonstration seems, rather, to have been that of a forum for farm leaders to express their grievances about the need to increase farm prices more drastically than the Commission had recommended.

The FNSEA moves on the Community level have been designed to make COPA more activist. Some of these moves have been within the framework of COPA; others have been undertaken independently. Examples of the FNSEA's activities on the Community level were the attempt to obtain the participation of the British National Farmers' Union and the German Farmers' Union in its "action day" in France on January 12, 1973; the "European" meeting of farmers in Valenciennes, France, on April 17, 1973; and the farm "summit meeting" called by FNSEA leaders for all European farm federations in Paris on September 3-4, 1974.[48]

These actions by the FNSEA were part of a strategy designed to turn COPA into an activist organization on the Community level. If sufficiently dynamic measures cannot be taken through COPA, the FNSEA has shown that it can take these steps without COPA and that it can achieve results. This is an unwelcome development for COPA leaders.

I can also mention under this heading the frequency of bilateral contacts that occur between national farm groups. The staffs of such organizations as the AGPB in Paris telephone their counterparts in Bonn and elsewhere frequently; there is no need to go through COPA for all contacts. Informal alliances form among national farm groups.

These developments obviously threaten COPA's position as the unique spokesman for the EC farm community. They will continue in the future, furthermore, because the forces producing them are growing stronger. The institutional development of COPA, the improvement in the quality of its proposals, and the increase in its staff and financial resources have not succeeded in lessening these dangers.

COPA AND EC POLICY MAKING

COPA has taken strong stands on two fundamental issues: the *manner* in which Community decisions are taken and the *substance* of those decisions. COPA has put forth surprisingly specific, long-range proposals on the way in which it wants to be involved in Community decisions; it has also, naturally, presented its views on the substance of farm policy. This section will examine both of these areas.

COPA has made many recommendations to improve the consultation process. V. O. Key has argued that interest groups become more particularistic with time, concentrating on short-term concerns.[49] Such does not seem to be the case with COPA, and its dogged insistence on changing the way in which it is consulted by EC institutions, especially by the Commission, is a good example of its tenacity in pursuing long-range goals.

From its inception, COPA has attempted to apply national methods of consultation between ministries of agriculture and farm groups to the EC decision-making process. The German practice of submitting an annual Green Report to the Bundestag, to become the subject of public debate, and the British annual review in which ministry and farm experts discuss the upcoming year's prices have been the most popular models for COPA leaders. They have attempted to put the consultation on a judicial basis, obliging the Commission to follow certain procedures in obtaining the farmers' position. The most important elements in this process are an annual report describing the status of EC agriculture for the previous year, especially the improvement or deterioration of farm income, and the annual price review.

COPA officials explain that one of the major reasons for formalizing the consultation process is that it imposes clear obligations on Community politicians, including Commission officials. Considerable distrust is expressed by COPA about the value of informal agreements and commitments undertaken by Commission or Council officials. In the farmers' eyes, the Community (as well as the national) politician craves ambiguity and tries to avoid being pinned down to specific goals. This reduces his freedom of maneuver. COPA leaders have therefore led a long campaign to institutionalize and formalize the consultative process. [50]

The second major policy concern involves substantive policies. In this discussion, questions of price, compensatory levies, and economic and monetary union will be examined.

The question of price policy is connected to other policy questions before the EC such as the desirability of economic and monetary union, the speed and shape of farm modernization, regional development, foreign trade, and, indeed, the EC's general relations with both the developed Western nations and the Third World. A decision on farm prices obviously governs the farmer's income. In fact, if there are no supplementary forms of aid to the farmer, the price decision governs the farmer's entire income from agricultural pursuits. If, as is the case in EC member states such as France and Germany, highly developed farms coexist with many marginal ones, price hikes can lead to a widening gap between rich and poor farmers. The former, with their modern operations designed to boost productivity when desired, can reap great profits when, for example, the price of their commodity is raised 5 percent. The latter, on the other hand, produce such a small amount of the commodity in question that they cannot expand production very much to take advantage of the price rise. An exclusive reliance on prices in farm policy, therefore, runs the risk of exacerbating divisions within the rural world, with all the political and social unrest that this would entail. [51]

A companion to price policy—and sometimes in the development of the common agricultural policy it seemed to be an alternative—is structural policy. This involves government aid to farmers to improve their operations. It can include a wide range of activities, such as consolidating land holdings to form bigger farms, use of machinery, introduction of training programs. It also almost necessarily involves measures for the reduction of the farm population. Numerous small farms cannot profitably use machinery under any conditions. Some small farms must logically disappear if larger farms are to result. Older farmers may not be able to embark on major improvement schemes. And most important from the government's standpoint, a reduction in the number of farmers may be one way to reduce farm surpluses. (However, modernization of the remaining farms will increase productivity and possibly create new surpluses.)

In Europe, discussions of structural reform usually entail resistance by large-scale farmers. Why is this so? They profit from a farm policy that relies mainly on high prices to ensure a decent farm income. In order to ensure a decent income for the marginal farmer, the price must be high enough for the extremely efficient farmer to reap a handsome profit. If supplementary aids are used to guarantee the marginal farmer's income during the period of transition to a smaller farm population, high prices are no longer necessary to fulfill this goal. (They may be necessary, of course, if the government desires to increase greatly the production of a given commodity.) Big farmers in European countries such as France and Germany have most often used their leadership positions in the farmers' organizations to fight structural policies and to rally the small farmers in this fight by portraying structural reform as the death knell of family farming. To a large extent, of course, this is true: Many of the small family farms in the Community will disappear in the next two decades. The question concerns how this social transformation will be accomplished. Structural-reform advocates argue that planning will smooth the difficulties of a change that is inevitable. For those farmers whose operations are more viable than the very small farms but are not on an extremely large scale, modernization programs such as the Mansholt Plan would make possible the adaptation necessary to survive.

The introduction of structural policies requires political courage: The government must face not only the wrath of the small farmers who will lose their livelihood but also the unwillingness of the big farmers to forsake high farm prices. The evolution of agricultural markets since 1972 has, in many ways, cut the ground out from under the reform movement. When Mansholt was drawing up his reform proposals and persuading the Council to adopt them, from 1967 to 1971, the EC faced mounting surpluses of wheat or beef or butter. These were caused by high prices, which were necessary in part because the small farmer's income depended solely on prices. Mansholt wanted to stop using price as the sole determinant of farm income, supplementing it with direct grants to poor farmers. This would permit prices to perform the function of matching supply with demand.

In 1972-73, however, the specter of burgeoning surpluses suddenly disappeared as bad weather, poor harvests, and mounting world demand for foodstuffs completely disoriented world food markets. Within months, EC food prices, previously higher than world prices, sank below them. In August-September 1972, EC wheat prices were double the world price; a year later they were 20 percent lower. The elaborate system of target prices and levies that had been designed to bolster Community food prices and tax food imports now functioned to stabilize food prices to the consumer and actually tax Community exports of food! In a reversal of alliances, wheat farmers in the EC complained as Brussels taxed grain exports in order to preserve the Community's supply, while the common agricultural policy found defenders in such unlikely persons as the British Minister of Agriculture.[52]

Under these conditions of world food shortages and high prices, pressure for drastic structural reform in the Community declined. Even Mansholt, in his resignation letter to the incoming president of the Commission in 1972, seemed to have second thoughts. The first condition for a stable world order, he wrote, was "priority to food production, by investing also in food products that are supposedly 'not profitable' to produce."[53] Mansholt also had reservations about abandoning large areas of Community farm land and swelling the urban population. The president of the French farmers' federation, Michel Debatisse, welcomed these statements, saying that the letter "would reassure [farmers] in their demands."[54]

It is against this background that the evolution of COPA's position on farm prices must be seen. The ability to present common demands for farm prices, supported by all member organizations, is also a measure of the ability of COPA to foster agreement among its national groups.

In general, COPA has constantly defended the family farm, a price policy that reflects production costs as well as the need to orient production, protection of EC markets, and structural and regional policies that increase productivity.[55]

COPA faced the greatest threats of dissension among its members when the first market organization was being formed in the area of grains in 1964-66. Here, the Germans opposed the other members, especially the French. On the next market regulations, setting up rules for milk products and beef, there was much more agreement; most producers tolerated or favored EC regulation in these product areas, though they may have desired higher prices. The beginning prices, however, did not involve major reductions in any national prices, as did the beginning wheat prices.[56] After the regulations had established the ground rules for marketing in each product sector, prices had to be set by the Council each spring. Finding agreement on price recommendations posed less intense problems for COPA than did the search for agreement on the basic market regulations themselves.

Figure 8 summarizes COPA's ability to reach agreement on price recommendations from 1966 through 1975. The graph depicts three levels of agreement, from failure to reach any common recommendation, through agreement on a general price increase or general principles for increasing prices, to agreement on specific price increases for each product. COPA's record of agreement is uneven, with a slump in 1970-71, the years during which debate over the Mansholt Plan was raging in farm circles. In 1970, for example French farmers did not request any price increases for wheat—their profitable operations probably permitted a satisfactory return. Besides, the Mansholt Plan was designed to correct just such inequities as exorbitant profits for wheat producers, and the French probably wanted to keep a low profile. The German wheat farmers, however, asked for a 5 percent increase—their operations were more expensive than those of their French counterparts.[57] As inflation hit farm markets in the 1970s, agreement seemed to become easier: Even if a national group desired only a 5 percent increase, why not agree with other groups in COPA that are pressing for a 10 percent increase? This has been the case with the German Farmers' Union in recent years: Although Germany has experienced lower rates

FIGURE 8

COPA's Ability to Reach Agreement on Price Recommendations, 1966-75

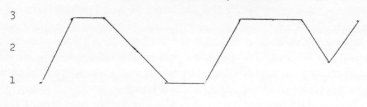

1966 1967 1968 1969 1970 1971 1972 1973 1974 1974 1975
                                                  interim
                                                  increase

1 = No Common Recommendation on Price Increase
2 = Agreement on General Level of Price Increase
3 = Agreement on Specific Price Increases by Product

Note: 1 = no common recommendation; 2 = agreement on a general price increase; 3 = agreement on specific price increases by product.

Sources: COPA, Presidium, minutes, October 20, 1967; "Prise de position du COPA en ce qui concerne la fixation des prix pour la campagne 1971-1972"; Presidium, minutes, October 1, 1971; Presidium, "Resolution," July 12, 1974; "COPA's Position Regarding the Farm Price Review for the Marketing Year 1975-76," December 6, 1974; *Agra-Europe*, May 5, 1966; October 26, 1967; November 28, 1968; May 29, 1969; April 1, 1971; February 15, 1973; June 17, 1974.

of inflation than France, the DBV could usually support high price demands in COPA; this was a painless form of agreement.[58]

The difficult aspect of reaching agreement on price recommendations inside COPA comes not on questions of the average price increase desired for all products but on the allocation of this price increase among products.[59] COPA has admitted the difficulties involved in allocating price increases, which concern "conflicts of interests between producers and users" of given commodities such as grains, which are a major input for livestock, poultry, and milk products.[60] Such conflicts stem from the conditions of production, and there is no solution for them except acceptable side payments by the Council in the form of direct grants to producers of certain commodities. And even this solution probably smacks too much of structural reform, with all its connotations of the extinction of family farms, for it to constitute an effective remedy. This type of conflict will persist, then, within COPA regardless of how much interaction of farm elites takes place. The important point is that COPA has been able to contain the conflict and still function as an effective interest group on the Community level.

In addition to the matter of prices *per se*, other questions touch the issue of farm income and production directly and are closely linked with price discussions inside COPA. Structural policy has already been mentioned. The monetary and economic disturbances of recent years raised two other issues that dominate farm debates in COPA and the EC in general: monetary compensation amounts (*montants compensatories*) and the fate of the project for economic and monetary union.

COPA has steadfastly maintained that it is impossible to separate price policy and structural policy. Prices themselves must be high enough to ensure an adequate income (in addition to orienting the type and amount of production). COPA emphasized the primacy of price in the early 1960s, when little was said of structural reform, and in the 1970s during the structural debate.* National or Community aid measures given directly to farmers cannot replace prices as the source of income: A Community price policy, based on an annual review, using a system of objective criteria, "is *an essential factor in the formation of farm incomes. A policy for providing aids cannot be a substitute for this.*"[61] On this issue, relative unanimity has always prevailed in COPA.

The more specific issue of monetary compensation amounts arose with the collapse of the monetary system of the West, as set up by the Bretton Woods agreements of 1944. The prices fixed by the Council of Ministers for the common agricultural policy are not expressed in terms of any member state's national currency but, rather, in a unit of account equal to the pre-1971 dollar (before devaluation). If a Community member devalued its currency, its farm exports would consequently drop in price by the amount of devaluation and the prices received by its farmers on the domestic market would increase by the amount of the devaluation. (The reverse would occur if a nation revalued its currency.) In 1969, Germany revalued the mark and faced the problem of permitting her farmers' incomes to drop by the amount of the revaluation. Soon afterward, France devalued and faced the problem of an inflationary rise in her farmers' incomes. In both cases, the national governments and the Council sealed off each national agricultural market from the rest of the Community, authorizing what in effect were border taxes and restitutions to ensure that French and German farm products moved through the Community according to the rates of exchange prevailing before the currency changes. The monetary compensation amounts sealing off the French and German markets terminated the free trade in farm products, which had barely begun in 1966.[62]

---

*See, for example, the Assembly resolution in 1964: "Prices must assure a satisfactory income to farmers in and of themselves." (COPA, *Prise de position sur la politique agricole dans la CEE* [Brussels: December: 1964], p. 1.) The same position was reaffirmed in the communiqué of January 25, 1971, after a meeting between the COPA Presidium and the president of the Commission.

These monetary compensation amounts were phased out over a two-year period, but in August 1971, the United States devalued the dollar. A period of great monetary instability ensued, eventually resulting in a system of floating exchange rates. The Bretton Woods system of fixed parities was dead. The EC was obliged to restore the compensatory payments, this time in an extremely complex version because the member states were unable to cause their currencies to float together.[63]

The fate of the monetary compensation amounts has pitted French farmers and the French Government on one side against German farmers and the German Government on the other. The German farmers refuse to accept a reduction in their income for the sake of monetary purity. French farmers (especially wheat producers) wish to exploit the competitive advantage that would follow a devaluation.

This conflict has persisted within COPA. The German Farmers' Union in early 1975, for example, opposed action by the Council designed to decrease the extent of the compensatory payments, while the French FNSEA congratulated Commissioner Petrus Lardinois for his role in steering through the Council the reduction in monetary compensation amounts.[64] COPA has however adopted a compromise position on compensatory payments. COPA cannot permit, ruled the Presidium, farmers of certain countries (that is, of countries that have revalued their currencies) to endure a loss of income because of economic, finanical, or monetary difficulties: "In the absence of fixed exchange rates, compensatory measures, especially at the border, are necessary."[65] On the issue of compensatory payments, as on price issues, national groups sided with their national governments. National cleavages defined the alliances within COPA because of the differential impact that a uniform Community policy on the issue in question would have on the political economy of each member state.

The final issue closely connected with farm production is the project for economic and monetary union in the Community. The Werner Report, resulting from the 1969 EC summit conference at the Hague, called for economic and monetary union by 1980. COPA had much earlier pointed out the vulnerability of the common agricultural policy to monetary instability. The monetary crisis beginning in 1969 proved COPA correct. Changing parities necessitated the system of monetary compensation amounts that effectively hamper free trade in farm products. Economic and monetary union was clearly impossible in these circumstances, and today it remains a distant goal with little concrete impact on farmers today.

COPA's performance in EC policy making has demonstrated a relatively sophisticated approach to major farm issues. With regard to the methods used by the Community institutions to take decisions and pursue policies, COPA has pursued a long-range goal of shaping the consultation methods of the Community, specifically of the Commission, with some success. With regard to the substance of Community farm decisions, COPA has an uneven record in making policy recommendations on prices, compensatory payments, and economic and monetary union. Its ability to present a united front on these issues remains circumscribed by the structural characteristics of farm production and the impact of national economies on farmers' welfare.

NOTES

1. Jean Meynaud and Dusan Sidjanski, *Science politique et intégration européenne* (Geneva: Institut d'Etudes Européennes, 1965), pp. 64-65.

2. Terkel T. Nielsen, "Notes on Interest Aggregation and Articulation in the European Community: C.O.P.A.," in *Symposium Europa: 1950-1970* (Bruges, Belgium: College of Europe, 1971), pp. 252-54.

3. Jean Meynaud and Dusan Sidjanski, *Les Groupes de pression dans la communauté européenne: 1958-1968* (Brussels: Institut d'Etudes Européennes, 1971), pp. 164-70.

4. Ibid., pp. 172 ff; Chantal Mathy, "Essai d'analyse politique du Comité des Organisations Professionnelles Agricoles de la CEE " (unpublished memoir, Louvain, 1968), pp. 33 ff.

5. COPA, *Rules of Procedure of COPA* (Brussels, May 11, 1973), pp. 2-3.

6. Pierre Le Roy, *L'Avenir du Marché Commun agricole* (Paris: Presses Universitaires de France, 1973), p. 102.

7. Commission of the European Communities, *The Agricultural Situation in the Community* (Brussels: November 27, 1974), Part I, p. 3.

8. COPA, *Rules*, p. 5.

9. *Agra-Europe*, November 9, 1971.

10. COPA, *Rules*, p. 9.

11. Interview, March 1975.

12. Letter from M. P. Clegg, National Farmers' Union, March 26, 1975. See also the special issue of *Paysans*, "Le Royaume Uni et la CEE: Comment trouver des éléments d'entente?" (April-May 1974).

13. Interviews, March 1975; COPA, *Structure COPA-COGECA* (Brussels, November 8, 1973), p. 1.

14. Nielsen, "Notes," p. 260.

15. COPA, *Structure*, p. 1.

16. *Agra-Europe*, April 12, 1973.

17. COPA, *Rules*, p. 6.

18. Interviews, January and March 1975.

19. Meynaud and Sidjanski, *Les Groupes de pression*, pp. 190-91.

20. Interview, March 1975.

21. E. Gazzo, discussion during Round Table on the EC Summit (Brussels: Institut d'Etudes Européennes, November 19, 1974).

22. COPA, Draft letter to president of the permanent representatives asking for contacts with the Council and the Committee of Permanent Representatives (Brussels, n.d. [1965?]).

23. Interview, October 1974.

24. *Agra-Europe*, January 21 and 28, 1974.

25. Jean Deleau, report to the *Assemblee Permanent des Chambres d'Agriculture*, "Compte Rendu, APCA, Session Extraordinaire, 76e, 4-5 septembre 1974," *Chambres d'Agriculture* 541-542 (1974): 35.

26. Interview, October 1974.

27. Interview, January 1975.

28. Interview, January 1975.

29. Meynaud and Sidjanski, *Science politique*, p. 78. The same point is made in the analysis by the Europa Institut, *Les Groupes de pression dans la C.E.E.* (Amsterdam: University of Amsterdam, 1965), p. 32.

30. The original plan was published as a Commission memorandum, *Mémorandum sur la réforme de l'agriculture dans la Communauté Economique Européenne* COM (68) 1000 (Brussels: Commission of the European Communities, December 18, 1968).

31. *Agra-Europe*, October 8, 1970.

32. Ibid., December 3, 1970.

33. Richard J. Mayne, *The Institutions of the European Community* (London:Chatham House, 1968), pp. 44-45; Stephen Holt, *The Common Market* (London: H. Hamilton, 1967), pp. 108-12. The ambiguities of the Commission's role are analyzed in Karlheinz Neunreither, "Transformation of a Political Role: Reconsidering the Case of the Commission of the European Communities," *Journal of Common Market Studies* 10 (1972): 233-48.

34. David Coombes, *Politics and Bureaucracy in the European Community* (London: Chatham House, 1970), pp. 235-37.

35. Michael Palmer, John Lambert, *et al. European Unity: A Survey of the European Organizations* (London: Chatham House, 1963), p. 169.

36. Karl Kaiser, "Europe and America: A Critical Phase," *Foreign Affairs* 52 (1974): 725-41; James O. Goldsborough, "France, the European Crisis and the Alliance," ibid., 538-55.

37. Alan Watson, *Europe at Risk* (London: George G. Harrap, 1972), p. 181.

38. Interview, October 1974.

39. Interview, January 1975.

40. Interview, February 1975.

41. *Agra-Europe*, February 12, 1970.

42. Ibid., July 12, 1972.

43. Ibid., October 19, 1972.

44. Interviews, February and March 1975; *Agra-Europe*, May 28, 1970.

45. Interview, October 1974.

46. Interview, June 1974; *Der Spiegel*, March 29, 1971; *Le Monde*, March 23-26, 1971; *Agra-Europe*, March 4 and 25, 1971.

47. Interview, June 1974.

48. *Le Monde*, January 12, April 18, 1973; ibid., August 21, 1974; *Agra-Europe*, December 21, 1972.

49. V. O. Key, *Politics, Parties, and Pressure Groups* (New York: T. Y. Crowell, 1960), p. 179.

50. Interview, December 1974.

51. John Marsh and Christopher Ritson, *Agricultural Policy and the Common Market* (London: Chatham House, 1971), p. 60; D. Bergmann *et al.*, *A Future for European Agriculture* (Paris: Atlantic Institute, 1970), pp. 12-13.

52. Jon McLin, "Europe's Common Agricultural Policy in a Time of Shortages," *American Universities Field Staff Reports*, West European Series, 8 (1973); Jon McLin, "Western Europe and the World Food Problem," ibid., 9 (1975).

53. Lawrence Deboue and Albert Te Pass, eds., *La Lettre Mansholt: Réactions et commentaries* (Paris: J. J. Pauvert, 1972), p. 13.

54. Ibid., p. 103.

55. Mathy, "Essai d'analyse politique," pp. 46 ff.

56. Interview, December 1974.

57. COPA, "Prise de position du COPA en ce qui concerne la fixation des prix pour la campagne 1971-72" (Brussels, November 26, 1970).

58. Interview, March 1975.

59. Interview, March 1975.

60. COPA, "Report on the Discussions of the Presidium on the Situation of the Common Agricultural Policy," July 13, 1973, p. 12.

61. COPA, "Report on the Discussions of the Presidium on the Situation of the Common Agricultural Policy," pp. 7-8. Emphasis in original.

62. Pierre Baudin, "Crises monétaires et politique agricole commune d'août 1969 à juillet 1973," *Revue du Marché Commun* (August-September 1973): 309-18.

63. Ibid.

64. COPA, Presidium, minutes, February 18, 1975.

65. COPA, "Prise de position du COPA sur la proposition de la Commission au Conseil concernant la fixation des prix agricoles de la campagne 1975-76 pour certains produits agricoles et certaines mésures connexes " (Brussels, January 9, 1975), p. 4.

CHAPTER

6

STRATEGIES OF
INFLUENCE

The establishment of the EC created another layer of political institutions with which national pressure groups had to deal. The national groups themselves formed Eurogroups in many economic sectors to deal with the institutions of the Community. The number of possible channels of influence has expanded greatly since 1958. In addition to national channels—the government, bureaucracy, parliament, and regulatory agencies—national groups may now choose to contact the European Commission, the Council of Ministers, the Committee of Permanent Representatives, their own Eurogroup, and so forth.

Earlier chapters dealt with these new channels in isolation, analyzing the national political systems, the national groups' reactions to EC initiatives, and the farmers' Eurogroup. It is not enough, however, simply to examine various channels. How do interest groups actually use these new channels?

The imposition of the layer of EC institutions and Eurogroups on the previously existing national systems has rendered complex patterns of politics in European states even more complex. Now we need to see how national groups use the various elements of the new system in new strategies of influence.

Four strategies of influence are presented in this chapter. They represent four ways in which the various elements of the EC decision-making system can be combined. The conditions under which these strategies can be used successfully are discussed together with the relative frequency with which they have in fact been used during the existence of the common agricultural policy.

Seen from a national interest group's perspective, the EC contains numerous institutional emements that may be used to influence policy outcomes. These elements may be combined in a variety of ways. One way is the more or less "orthodox" way laid down in the Rome Treaty and in Commission statements. But, as will be seen, this is not the only way of combining these elements.

An analysis of the conditions under which one strategy is chosen in preference to another will help to explain the dynamics of interest-group politics in the Community: Why, for example, is COPA sometimes bypassed? When do purely national channels in the EC system give the greatest promise of success? When do national groups choose to evade the EC system entirely?

If we consider the institutional structure of the EC and the connections between the EC institutions and national institutions, all of which compose what we term the EC system, it is clear that the following elements can be used by national groups: national interest group, COPA, Commission, national government, Council of Ministers.[1] These elements are nodes in a network of influence, and the possible linkages are shown in Figure 9.

FIGURE 9

Possible Linkages in EC Network

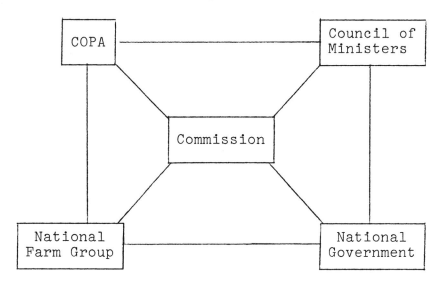

Not all of these possible relationships are used at any one time. Under certain conditions, a specific combination of nodes will be used in a certain strategy of influence. Four major strategies are discussed below, together with examples of their use. The conditions under which each strategy is probable are given. Finally, some general considerations about the relative importance of the nodes are given.

THE ORTHODOX STRATEGY

This strategy is the one provided by the usual workings of the EC as described by the Rome Treaty and official Commission statements. The Commission draws up proposals. In order to influence the Commission, national farm organizations must act through COPA because the Commission refuses to negotiate officially with national interest groups. In order to influence the final stage of decision making in the Council, the national organizations return to the national scene and explain their case to their national governments. This process is depicted in Figure 10. The numbers indicate the temporal order in which the actions are taken.

FIGURE 10

The Orthodox Strategy

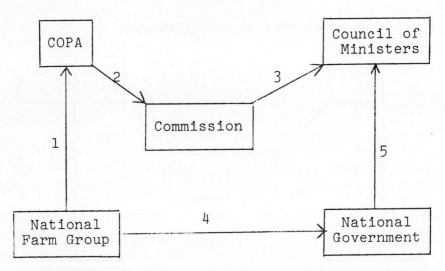

From the comments made in Chapter 5, it is clear that Community decision making does not always fit this pattern. Sometimes national groups approach the Commission or even the Council directly, and so on. In order for this orthodox strategy to be used, these conditions must obtain:

1. The national group must be a member of COPA. As we have seen, a growing number of farm groups do not belong to COPA.
2. The national group must find COPA's final position sufficiently agreeable to allow COPA to represent the national group vis-a-vis the Commission, instead of trying to approach the Commission directly.

3. The Commission must be willing to deal with COPA and eschew contacts with national interest groups. But the Commission, as we have seen, often has conflicting goals; for example, it may want to respect the role of COPA as sole farm spokesman but at the same time attempt to build a constituency for new programs by going directly to national groups, as Mansholt did when defending his structural-reform plan from 1968 to 1972.

4. The national group must have access to the national government, especially to the national Ministry of Agriculture. This is not true for all groups in Germany or France. In Germany, the Part-Time Farmers' Union (DBLN) is not yet considered a valid farm spokesman; in France, only the national federation (FNSEA) and the young farmers' CNJA are considered representative and hence consulted regularly by the government, while official access is denied groups such as MODEF and Paysans-Travailleurs on the left and the FFA and GEA on the right.

The orthodox strategy has been followed in most of the EC annual price decisions. It lends itself to issues that do not demand urgent action outside routine decision-making channels. Although the initial drawing up of the general market regulations (especially the grain regulations) often provoked severe dissension within COPA, the annual price negotiations usually prompted national groups to present their demands to the Commission by means of a COPA united front.

THE EMERGENCY STRATEGY

A less routine strategy, this approach is employed when fast action is needed and when the Commission is unwilling to grant the request. In this strategy, COPA is used to coordinate the action of individual national groups in approaching their national ministers in order to ensure that the same demands are presented, stressing the farmers' unity. As can be seen from Figure 11, when COPA's approaches to the Commission are refused, COPA is then used by national groups to coordinate their demands to their respective national ministers. The ministers can then insist that the Commission give serious consideration to COPA's initial demands. When the Commission finally submits its proposal to the Council, the ministers can grant the national groups some or all of their requests.

In order for this strategy to be effective, the following conditions are necessary:

1. The Commission must initially refuse a COPA request that seems fairly reasonable to most political elites involved in EC affairs.

2. The COPA position must retain member support when the coordinated approaches are made to the national ministers.

FIGURE 11

The Emergency Strategy

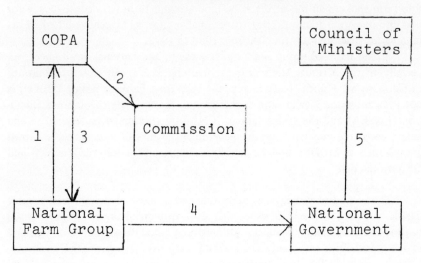

3. The national ministers must be persuaded that the farmers' demands are reasonable and merit overriding the Commission's reluctance to act. The institutional balance in the Community has shifted against the Commission sufficiently so that the Council has little hesitation in doing this.

4. The ministers must be able to convince the Commission to reverse its previous refusal to come forth with an emergency proposal. Whether the Council is successful depends in large part on the desire of commissioners, especially the agricultural commissioner, to defy Council wishes. Legally, the Council cannot force the Commission to put forward a specific kind of proposal.

A prime example of the emergency strategy is the special session of the Council in September 1974 that granted an interim price increase to farmers for the first time in EC history. In spite of the 8 percent price increase granted by the Council in the spring of 1974, severe inflation had seriously eroded farm incomes so that by July 1974 COPA had demanded that Commissioner Lardinois call a special Council session to consider an additional price increase.

During this meeting, Presidium members expressed to Lardinois their fears of growing farm unrest throughout the Community. The Germans in particular were apprehensive: Two days before, at a farmers' march in Munich, in which the German Farmers' Union estimated 6,000 farmers would participate, 30,000 farmers flocked to the Bavarian capital.[2] This specific indication of unrest was produced by much deeper forces that threatened to break up the entire common agricultural policy. In May the Italian Government had blocked free imports from other EC countries, requiring all Italian importers to deposit 50 percent of the value of the goods to be imported in interest-free bank accounts for six months—in effect, a tax on imports. The Italian move struck at the heart of the entire Community system, endangering the system of free trade that had been so laboriously constructed. It struck in particular at French and German food sales to Italy. (In 1973, France sold more than a billion dollars worth of food products to Italy, especially beef.)[3] By the spring of 1974, the beef market in the EC was already suffering; prices were collapsing under the pressure of surplus production and continued beef imports from Eastern Europe and Latin America. In Germany, Bavaria was especially hard hit by the Italian move; almost two-thirds of German food exports to Italy came from Bavaria.[4]

All this lay behind the Presidium's concern for urgent measures from the Community. With the common agricultural policy unable to function, farmers would turn to their national governments for aid. However, while COPA leaders were concerned about protecting the farmers' incomes, Lardinois, Mansholt's successor as agriculture commissioner, was preoccupied with ending the growing distortions to competition. The Presidium meeting with the commissioner ended stormily with Lardinois refusing to request a special meeting of the Council and with the farm leaders angrily retorting that he should not be surprised by outbreaks of rural violence during the summer.[5]

That same day, COPA leaders considered alternatives. The Presidium sent a telegram to Christian Bonnet, the French Agriculture Minister who was president of the Council during the second half of 1974, asking him to convene the Council earlier than its scheduled September 23 meeting. It was decided that all COPA delegates would ask their respective national ministers to call a Council meeting earlier than September 23. A suggestion was made to coordinate roadblocks throughout the Community to explain farmers' grievances to the public. It was pointed out, with the bloody mass demonstration of March 1971 no doubt serving as a warning, that the public simply would not tolerate another mass demonstration in Brussels.[6]

COPA did little during the month of August, when most of the initiative passed into the hands of the national groups, pressuring their national leaders.

In France, the traditional holiday month of August was marked by tension. The riots and demonstrations that swept the country showed both the weaknesses in the national farm federation as well as the federation's close workings with the French Government, which exposed it to fierce attacks from the right and the left. Already in July, Bonnet and Debatisse, the president of the FNSEA, had issued calls for order on the same day.[7] Although Paris had taken emergency measures to aid beef producers, the farmers were unsatisfied. They obeyed the calls of the dissident farm groups to demonstrate, making it impossible for the government to control the mass of farmers through the traditional, accredited farm organizations such as the FNSEA and the CNJA. The farmers wrecked prefectures, carried on *ventes sauvages* (direct sales to consumers), destroyed fruit trees, and set up roadblocks.[8]

In Germany, the Farmers' Union's national committee met on July 4 to discuss how to win higher prices for German farmers. Farm leaders were impressed by civil servants' pay raises and vowed to obtain similar benefits. A peaceful demonstration was ordered for early September.[9] The big Munich march at the end of July has already been mentioned. German farmers did not react as violently as French, Belgian, or Dutch farmers because the German rate of inflation was appreciably lower (half that of France).[10] The rural unrest was sufficiently grave, however, for Ertl to defend the German Farmers' Union against critics within and outside the Bonn government:

> The German Farmers' Union, in spite of all kinds of difficulties, is trying to maintain a fruitful dialogue with the government and prefers a policy of negotiations to a policy of demonstrations. We must support the president of the Farmers' Union in this policy.[11]

In Bonn as in Paris, the national farm organizations were useful to the government as keepers of order in the farm world. As Baron von Feury, vice-president of the DBV and its representative in the COPA Presidium, said in the middle of the summer, "We can no longer keep our legions calm."[12]

The farmers succeeded in obtaining a special Council session in early September, largely as a result of concerted Dutch-French moves, against the backdrop of widespread farm unrest in Belgium, the Netherlands, and France. In mid-August the Dutch Minister of Agriculture, Alfons Van der Stee met his French counterpart, Bonnet, in Paris to discuss the crisis. Dutch farmers, breaking their tradition of peaceful consultation with the government, had also demonstrated against falling prices and rising input costs during the summer. Van der Stee asked Bonnet, as president of the EC Council, to call a meeting for late August. Already, President Giscard d'Estaing had met French farm leaders and initimated that he would favor an early Council meeting. Bonnet was authorized to call a Council session on September 3, to be held in Paris.[13]

The Council meeting was in fact held September 3; it was the first in a series of meetings that eventually granted an interim price increase of 5 percent to supplement the annual increase passed the previous spring. (The final decision was not taken until the German "veto" of the price increase had been removed by a compromise according to which the Commission would undertake a reassessment of the common agricultural policy with a view to making it more efficient.)

The interim price increase of 1974 is a good example of the use of the emergency strategy by farm leaders. The initial approach to the Commission through COPA in the summer proved unsuccessful. Farm leaders then mapped out their approach to the national ministries within the COPA Presidium. The demonstrations of the summer put pressure on key governments of the Community, especially the Dutch and French governments. Furthermore, the lucky coincidence that France held the presidency of the Council at a time when

French farmers were demanding relief increased the probability that farm leaders, led by the French FNSEA, would obtain the special Council session.

The emergency strategy is clearly effective only when all farmers can defend a common COPA position. (And in the case of a price increase, even those farmers who have not been gravely hurt by inflation, such as the Germans, may defend the common demands because they have nothing to lose from a price increase.) A different situation arises, however, when the grievances affect only one EC state. An EC solution to a national problem can be obtained by means of the third strategy.

AN EC SOLUTION TO A NATIONAL GRIEVANCE

This strategy is especially interesting because it illustrates how, given the right conditions, national leaders can foist on the EC a policy designed mainly to solve the problems of one nation. This does not refer to various ad hoc measures granted by the Community, such as subsidies given to German farmers from the EC Farm Fund after the December 1964 grain accords lowered German farm prices. Rather, it concerns the adoption by the EC of measures applicable to all member states, even though the impetus for such measures comes from the interest groups and political leaders of one state. Under this strategy, portrayed in Figure 12, the national interest group convinces its minister of the need for action. The minister, with the sanction of the national government, then persuades his colleagues within the Council of Ministers that such a relief measure should be granted. The Council then prevails upon the Commission to come forth with the necessary proposal, which the Council then passes. It should be noted that the Council's pressure on the Commission to produce a specific proposal is completely informal and unofficial; legally, the Council cannot dictate to the Commission the specific policies contained within a proposal.

The conditions necessary for the success of this strategy are rather special:

1. The national group must have great political importance for the national government.
2. The national minister must be willing and able to lobby strongly within his government for the group's demands.
3. The national government must permit an extremely demanding stand by its minister inside the Council of Ministers.
4. The Commission must submit to the urging of the Council to come forth with the required proposal.

These conditions appear stringent, and yet they have existed several times in the past few years, permitting a national group to use this strategy with effect. The most important example of this strategy was the revision of the market-

FIGURE 12

An EC Solution to a National Grievance

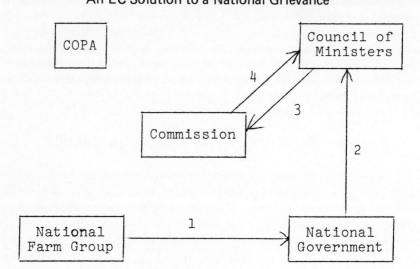

intervention system for beef within the EC. It will be recalled that the market regulations for beef were much weaker than those for wheat. The latter assurred the producer of a certain price for his wheat, and the collecting agencies were obliged to purchase all quantities delivered to them. In this way, the wheat producer had a solid floor price for his production. The beef producer was in quite a different situation. The producer sold his animals to slaughterhouses, which in turn graded and slaughtered the animals. The minimum beef price was simply a target price, not a guaranteed price. When the market price fell to 98 percent of the target price throughout the EC, and to 93 percent of the target price in at least one region of the EC, the stocking agents would begin buying up beef from processors. This emergency purchase of beef would, it was hoped, increase the prices received by the beef producers.[14]

It is obvious that this intervention system was not nearly as satisfactory to the beef producer as the wheat system to the wheat farmer. The beef system relied on the play of market forces, bolstered by temporary Community purchases, to increase the beef price, whereas the intervention agencies for wheat made a standing offer to purchase all supplies of wheat at the Community intervention price. The beef producer was not guaranteed any specific price; he simply had the assurance that the beef intervention agencies would begin purchasing limited supplies of beef when the prices in the Community as a whole and the producer's specific region fell below a certain level.

The situation of the beef producers in the EC varied greatly. The French producers were the most dissatisfied with this system. Relations between producers and processors in France were strained, the producers charging that the processors manipulated the market, giving producers the worst possible prices through unfair contracts. In Germany, on the other hand, relations between producers and processors were quite different. As a Commission official observed:

> In Germany, the system of *Versandschlachtereien* [forwarding slaughterhouses] buys animals from the producer and pays him the amount remaining after a certain amount of profit is deducted from the Community intervention price. France does not have this system, and you might say that the processing system there is not as honest as the German system, hence the continual unrest among French beef producers.[15]

French beef producers in particular, therefore, understandably desired the stability of the wheat intervention system.

The French beef producers were mainly small farmers, concentrated in the poorer regions of southern and western France. The discontent of these farmers was growing in the early 1970s, benefiting MODEF, the Communist-oriented farm group.[16] This posed a threat to the unity of the national farm federation, which alarmed the government. For this reason, and also because it wished to develop French beef production in order to capture a growing European market, Paris was receptive to improvements in the beef sector.

In addition to these general forces of change, the character of the newly appointed Agriculture Minister in 1972 increased the probability of rapid action for beef farmers. The Minister of Agriculture was Chirac, who was in his first major cabinet post. He was determined to make his name as the youngest Agriculture Minister of the Fifth Republic. Chirac's ambition fitted in nicely with the beef producers' demands for help. He pledged to his clientele that a solution would be found.[17]

Chirac gained the support of the French Government for his project to change the EC beef intervention system. It would be, after all, an inexpensive victory for Paris because much of the financial burden of intervention would be shared by other states through the EC Farm Fund. The Council of Ministers prodded the Commission to produce a proposal altering the intervention system, which was adopted by the Council on December 28, 1972. Under the new system, intervention became permanent, as it was for wheat: It "involves the purchase at predetermined prices of beef and veal . . . which may be put up for sale at any time."[18] This beef intervention system was combined with a new Beef Office within France to pacify French beef producers and ensure their support of the regime in the legislative elections of March 1973.

The way in which this decision was taken is important because it diverged so sharply from the stereotyped image of Community decision making. As one COPA official pointed out:

The change in the beef intervention system was really an enormous achievement by Chirac. Both Pompidou and Chirac came from Correze, a livestock region, and legislative elections were approaching. Chirac was able to convince the Council to take this step, and the Council forced the Commission to withdraw its earlier proposition and come back with the one Chirac wanted.[19]

This was a case of EC decision making in which COPA was absent and the Council took the initiative, prodded by one of its most dynamic members.

RETREAT TO NATIONAL MEASURES

This strategy might, at first glance, seem to be merely a continuation of national politics as usual, but it is, compared to the strategy just discussed, an even more extreme case of the nationalization of EC politics. It represents, in fact, the retreat of national interest groups and governments to the realm of purely national measures to counter the harmful effects of EC policies or to substitute national policies for existing or envisaged EC policies.

Such nationalization of the common agricultural policy has increased greatly since 1970. It represents governments' unwillingness to permit the common agricultural policy to operate on farm constituencies untrammeled by any national safety measures or guidelines. The disorder in the world monetary system, rampant inflation, skyrocketing energy costs, and uncertain commodity markets have meant that national governments have been obliged to grant questionable national aids to farmers in times of crisis. The EC decision-making process usually requires too much time for national governments to use it when rural regions erupt into violence. For governments such as the French, which must be constantly on guard against a coalescence of peasant and labor discontent, national measures represent a sure and reliable safety valve.

To be sure, many national measures are permitted by the Commission, which must rule on all such measures. Often, a mere manipulation of legal niceties (in which the common agricultural policy abounds) makes the difference between the Commission's approval or disapproval of national measures. This seems to have been the case in the summer of 1974, when the Commission decided to bring France before the Court of Justice of the EC because of certain aids granted to her farmers, while Belgium granted substantially the same type of aid but escaped censure.[20] What is distressing for advocates of the common agricultural policy, however, is the near tripling of such national measures from 1973 to 1974, indicating the extreme distress of the Community's farmers and the willingness of most Community governments to seek immediate national remedies. In 1973, 66 aid schemes were submitted by national governments to the Commission for its approval. The following year, the figure rose to 165.

Most of this increase was caused by the need to meet higher energy costs, which raised the prices of the farmer's fertilizer, tractor fuel, and so forth. The Commission usually approved such measures if they were temporary.[21]

A more serious nationalization of farm policy in the Community is represented by Germany's Individual Farm Promotion Scheme and Complementary Social Programme (*Einzelbetriebliches Förderungs- und soziales Ergänzungs-programm für die Land-und Forstwirtschaft*), dubbed the Ertl Plan after Bonn's Agriculture Minister. This plan is, in effect, Bonn's answer to Brussel's Mansholt Plan to modernize Europe's agriculture while drastically reducing its farm population.

The Rome Treaty does not specifically call for a Community program of structural reform, and the EC member states have jealously guarded this area of agricultural policy. The resistance of most Community farmers and national governments to the Mansholt Plan for structural reform has been mentioned frequently. Although Mansholt was able to obtain support for his plan from some quarters in France, especially from the reformist farmers of the CNJA, opposition in Germany to the plan was practically unanimous. At the end of 1970 all parties in the Bundestag rejected the Mansholt Plan. Chancellor Brandt emphasized that structural questions were a national, not a Community, problem and would be handled by the national authorities.[22]

Ertl announced his own modernization plan in 1970, promoting it as an alternative to Mansholt's project. The German Farmers' Union was remarkably calm about Ertl's plan, which used the techniques advocated by Mansholt while departing from the philosophy of the Mansholt reform. Ertl kept the two basic parts of the Mansholt project: To receive aid, farmers must, first, keep adequate financial records and, second, submit a development plan showing how they intended to create a profitable farm within a given number of years. The difference between the Ertl Plan and the Mansholt Plan lay in the sizes of the farms that would be aided. Mansholt wanted to aim for the establishment of large farms throughout the Community by 1980; Ertl wanted to preserve the medium-sized farms also. Ertl also included in his plan a system of compensation that approached the system used by the British, whereby "deficiency payments" were paid to farmers to supplement the market price when that price was judged too low to provide a decent income.

The Ertl Plan was passed in late 1970 and went into effect January 1, 1971. It was adapted to Community regulations in 1973, but it remains a national program satisfying national objectives. The Ertl Plan received the quiet support of the Farmers' Union president, who perhaps saw in it a less drastic alternative to the Mansholt Plan. The introduction of a deficiency-payments scheme (which the Community had supposedly renounced) was also no doubt comforting to the farm leadership because it provided a buffer against possible unfavorable price policy from Brussels.[23]

The Ertl Plan is significant because it represented a turning back from the possibility that the Community might embark on a program of structural reform. German farmers opposed the specific form that the Community initiative, shaped by Mansholt, took; and the German government opposed the loss of power to Brussels that the adoption of such a program would have represented. As early as the Hague Conference in December 1969, Brandt had reaffirmed the national character of structural measures in agriculture. The adoption of the plan put forth by Ertl was therefore a retreat from supranational to national policy, and the permissive, if not openly favorable, attitude of the German farm leadership to the Ertl Plan is a good illustration of the fourth type of interest-group strategy, in which Community channels are renounced for the more comfortable national ones.

THE SIGNIFICANCE OF THE FOUR STRATEGIES

This presentation of four types of strategies that national interest groups may use in the Community decision-making system is important for several reasons. First, and most obvious, it shows that the "official" strategy found in the Rome Treaty and espoused by the Commission is not the only one which is in fact used. Interest groups use other strategies, depending on the receptivity of the different institutions to their cases, the importance of the interest groups themselves in national political systems, and national groups' access to the Eurogroup.

Second, this analysis permits a judgment about COPA's relative importance in the Community decision-making system. COPA plays a key role in the "official" strategy because it is the sole legitimate spokesman for Community farmers. COPA is also important in the second strategy, the emergency strategy. But COPA's importance in the second strategy is not based on its officially sanctioned role as sole farm spokesman, as is the case in the first strategy. Rather, it is important because it is a convenient forum in which farm leaders can plan a common set of demands to be presented to their national ministers and governments. In the third and fourth strategies, COPA is absent because the national interest group is either using its national government to push a certain measure through the Council or turning away from Community institutions altogether.

Finally, this analysis permits some cautious predictions about the fate of COPA in the future. Earlier chapters have depicted the growing institutional strength of COPA. The present chapter puts this increasing strength in context. If the Community continues to experience difficulties in maintaining the common agricultural policy intact, if national governments resort to national measures more and more, if the national groups must resort more frequently to approaching the Council through their national governments in order to persuade the Commission to make certain proposals, then COPA's overall importance as a Eurogroup can only decline.

NOTES

1. Several writers have outlined the possible channels of influence that national interest groups can use, but they have not considered the different ways in which these channels can be combined or the different conditions that give rise to different combinations. See Terkel T. Nielsen, "Aspects of the EEC Influence of European Groups in the Decision-Making Process: The Common Agricultural Policy," *Government and Opposition* 6 (Autumn 1971): 539-58; Wilhelm Gieseke, "Die berufsständischen Organisationen der Landwirtschaft in der agrarpolitischen Willensbildung der EWG," in *Agrarpolitik in der EWG*, Theodor Dams *et al.* eds. (Munich: Bayerischer Landwirtschaftsverlag, 1968), pp. 209-20. A perceptive attempt to weigh the relative importance of different channels is Werner J. Feld, "National Economic Interest Groups and Policy Formation in the EEC," *Political Science Quarterly* 80 (1966): 392-411.

2. COPA, Presidium, minutes, July 30, 1974; *Agra-Europe*, August 1, 1974.

3. *Le Monde*, May 3, 1974.

4. *Agra-Europe*, May 9, 1974.

5. COPA, Presidium, minutes, July 30, 1974; interview, September 1974.

6. COPA, Presidium, minutes, July 26, 1974.

7. *Le Monde*, July 25, 1974.

8. Ibid.

9. *Agra-Europe*, June 27, July 11, 1974.

10. *Frankfurter Allgemeine Zeitung*, August 5, 1974.

11. *Agra-Europe*, August 22, 1974.

12. *Stern*, July 18, 1974, p. 88.

13. *Le Monde*, August 11-12, 13, 31, September 1-2, 1974; *Herald Tribune*, August 1, 2, 3-4, 1974; *Agra-Europe*, August 22, 1974.

14. Commission of the European Economic Community, *Second General Report on the Activities of the European Economic Community* (Brussels, 1968), pp. 154-55.

15. Interview, March 1975. See also John Ardagh, *The New French Revolution* (New York: Harper & Row, 1969), pp. 85-87.

16. Adrien Zeller, *L'Imbroglio agricole du Marché Commun* (Paris: Calmann-Levy, 1970), pp. 73-74.

17. *Le Monde*, May 26-27, 28, 1974.

18. Commission of the European Communities, *Seventh General Report on the Activities of the European Communities* (Brussels, 1974), p. 271.

19. Interview, March 1975.

20. *Le Monde*, August 2, 1974.

21. Commission of the European Communities, *Eighth General Report* (Brussels, 1975), pp. 153-54.

22. *Agra-Europe*, November 12, 1970.

23. On the development of the Ertl Plan, see Josef Ertl, *Ernährungs- und Landwirtschaftspolitik: 1969 bis 1972* (Bonn: Bundesministerium für Ernährung, Landwirtschaft und Forsten, 1972), pp. 16 ff.; Organization for Economic Cooperation and Development, *Agricultural Policy in Germany* (Paris: The Organization, 1974), pp. 41 ff.; Organization for Economic Cooperation and Development, *Structural Reform Measures in Agriculture* (Paris: The Organization, 1972).

CHAPTER

7

CONCLUSION

Conventional integration theory assigned interest groups a crucial role in the process of constructing a supranational political system. This analysis of key agricultural interest groups on the national and European levels has been an attempt to judge whether such a role has in fact been performed. If it has not been performed in the agricultural sector of the European Community, which has seen the strongest development of supranational policies at the expense of the national governments, it will probably not be performed by interest groups in those integration projects that have developed more slowly and less successfully.

Two questions were asked at the outset: Why did national interest groups respond in certain ways to integration in their economic sectors? On the Community level, has the agricultural Eurogroup founded by national interest groups assumed the functions that were formerly performed by national groups?

After a review of the common agricultural policy and the institutional context in which it was established, the farm politics of two member states, France and Germany, were examined. The development of COPA, the major farm Eurogroup, was assessed, together with the possibilities of its future growth. The following conclusions emerge from the study.

Community agricultural policy was formulated not on a *tabula rasa* but, rather, against a backdrop of long traditions, entrenched interests, established national farm groups, and powerful government marketing organizations. These elements were subsumed under, but not eliminated by, the common agricultural policy. In particular, the electoral salience of farm issues in national systems has meant that Community farm policy has had to proceed slowly in rearranging the patterns of national farm politics. National bureaucratic ties have, in some cases, been supplemented by EC ties, as Eurogroups have constructed links with the EC bureaucracies, chiefly the Commission. National party ties, however, have no counterpart on the EC level; and national groups continue to cultivate their ties with national parties in order to influence the top leaders of their national governments. And because the links between national farm groups, national parties, and national marketing organizations (which implement the Community's price policy) have remained, the national system is ready to resume functioning if the Community's farm policy collapses. This, indeed, is the specter haunting Brussels in the late 1970s. Political integration, even in an area such as agriculture, which has seen major elements of supranationality, is eminently reversible.

National interest groups do not automatically support or oppose integration in their economic sectors. Their stands depend on the extent to which they perceive integration as furthering their own goals. The goals of national farm groups have generally been satisfactory prices and a market organization that guarantees that the farmers actually receive the prices set by the national or Community institutions.

The Eurogroup founded by national farm groups, COPA, has grown in resources and institutional complexity in order to deal with the increasing complexity of the common agricultural policy and the Community decision-making process. COPA has assumed one important function that national farm groups cannot perform in the Community: It can claim to be the sole legitimate spokesman for Community farmers and as such the only professional farm group qualified to present farmers' demands to the Commission. COPA's legitimacy has been damaged in recent years, however, as discontent with COPA, with the common agricultural policy, and with the Community in general has driven some farmers to form a second Eurogroup, COMEPRA. This splintering of farm groups on the Community level is paralleled on the national level. France and, to a lesser extent, Germany have experienced fragmentation of their farm organizations, rendering the task of the national ministries of agriculture more difficult as the ability of farm leaders to persuade the rank and file has diminished.

The elites that have dominated national farm groups are the same elites that dominate COPA, and COPA's preoccupation with price policy to the disadvantage of structural policy has simply reflected the priorities of national farm leaders.

COPA has attempted, with some success, to duplicate on the Community level the consultation procedures practiced by national governments, especially the German and British governments. COPA's aim is the restriction of the freedom of maneuver of Community officials by persuading them to commit themselves to the attainment of certain goals and the use of certain procedures.

National interest groups have several strategies open to them in attempting to influence Community policy. COPA is most important in the "official" strategy according to which national groups draw up common requests inside

COPA, which then presents them to the Commission in order to influence its proposals to the Council. Other strategies are used, however, which permit national interest groups to bypass COPA (and even the Commission).

The nationalization of the common agricultural policy and of Community politics in general has increased since the enlargement of the Community. It has posed an indirect threat to COPA's mission, especially to the extent that the Commission's importance in the Community's decision-making structure declines and that of the Council increases even further. National channels of access become increasingly important, and national groups may have less incentive to work through COPA in the future.

BOOKS

Ackermann, Paul. *Der Deutsche Bauernverband im politischen Kraftspiel der BRD*. Tübingen: J. C. B. Mohr, 1970.

Alting von Geusau, F. A. M. *Beyond the European Community*. Leyden: A. W. Sijthoff, 1969.

Ardagh, John. *The New French Revolution*. New York: Harper & Row, 1969.

Association Générale des Producteurs de Blé. *AGPB. 1924-1974*. Paris: Editions Erick Grand, 1974.

Barral, Pierre. *Les agrariens français de Méline à Pisani*. Paris: Armand Colin, 1968.

Bergmann, D., et al. *A Future for European Agriculture*. Paris: Atlantic Institute, 1970.

Bethusy-Huc, Gräfin von. *Demokratie und Interessenpolitik*. Wiesbaden: Franz Steiner, 1962.

Breitling, Rupert. *Die Verbände in der Bundesrepublik*. Meisenheim: Glan, 1955.

Britton, D. K. *Cereals in the U.K.: Production, Marketing, and Distribution*. London: Pergamon Press, 1969.

Butterwick, Michael, and Edmund Neville-Rolfe. *Agricultural Marketing and the EEC*. London: Hutchinson, 1971.

Camps, Miriam. *European Unification in the Sixties*. New York: McGraw-Hill, 1966.

Clerc, François. *Le Marché Commun agricole*. Paris: Presses Universitaires de France, 1965.

Coombes, David. *Politics and Bureaucracy in the European Community* London: Chatham House, 1970.

Corti, Mario. *Politique agricole et construction de l'Europe*. Brussels: Etablissements Emile Bruylant, 1971.

Dams, Theodor, et al., eds. *Agrarpolitik in der EWG*. Munich: Bayerischer Landwirtschaftsverlag, 1968.

Debatisse, Michel. *La Révolution silencieuse*. Paris: Calmann-Levy, 1963.

Delorme, Hélène, and Yves Tavernier. *Les Paysans français et l'Europe*. Paris: Fondation Nationale des Sciences Politiques, 1969.

Ehrmann, Henry, ed. *Interest Groups on Four Continents*. Pittsburgh: University of Pittsburgh Press, 1958.

Ellwein, Thomas. *Das Regierungsystem der BRD*. Cologne: Westdeutscher Verlag, 1965.

Ertl, Josef. *Ernährungs- und Landwirtschaftspolitik: 1969 bis 1972*. Bonn: Bundesministerium für Ernährung, Landwirtschaft und Forsten, 1972.

Estievenart, Georges. *Les Partis politiques en Allemagne fédérale*. Paris: Presses Universitaires de France, 1973.

Europa Institut. *Les Groupes de pression dans la C.E.E.*. Amsterdam: University of Amsterdam, 1965.

Faure, Marcel. *Les Paysans dans la société française*. Paris: Armand Colin, 1966.

Fauvet, Jacques, and Henri Mendras, eds. *Les Paysans et la politique*. Paris: Armand Colin, 1958.

Franklin, S. H. *The European Peasantry: The Final Phase*. London: Methuen, 1969.

Gerschenkron, Alexander. *Bread and Democracy in Germany*. New York: Howard Fertig, 1966.

Grosser, Alfred. *Germany in Our Time: A Political History of the Postwar Years*. New York: Praeger, 1971.

Hallett, G. *The Social Economy of West Germany*. London: Macmillan, 1973.

Hanrieder, Wolfram F. *The Stable Crisis: Two Decades of German Foreign Policy*. New York: Harper & Row, 1970.

Holt, Stephen. *The Common Market*. London: H. Hamilton, 1967.

Johnson, Nevil. *Government in the Federal Republic of Germany: The Executive at Work*. Oxford, England: Pergamon Press, 1973.

Key, V. O. *Politics, Parties, and Pressure Groups*. New York: T. Y. Crowell, 1960.

Klatzmann, J. *Les politiques agricoles: Idées fausses et illusions*. Paris: Presses Universitaires de France, 1972.

Kolodziej, Edward. *French International Policy Under de Gaulle and Pompidou*. Ithaca, N.Y.: Cornell University Press, 1974.

Lambert, Bernard. *Les Paysans dans la lutte des classes*. Paris: Editions du Seuil, 1970.

LaPalombara, Joseph. *Politics Within Nations*. Englewood Cliffs, N.J.: Prentice-Hall, 1974.

Leitholf, Andres. *Das Einwirken der Wirtschaftsverbände auf die Agrarmarkt-organisation der EWG*. Baden-Baden: Nomos Verlagsgesellschaft, 1971.

LeRoy, Pierre. *L'Avenir du Marché Commun agricole*. Paris: Presses Universitaires de France, 1973.

Macridis, Roy C. *French Politics in Transition: The Years After de Gaulle*. Cambridge, Mass.: Winthrop, 1975.

Malgrain, Yves. *L'Intégration agricole dans l'Europe des Six*. Paris: Editions Cujas, 1965.

Mansholt, Sicco. *La Crise*. Paris: Editions Stock, 1974.

Marsh, John, and Christopher Ritson. *Agricultural Policy and the Common Market*. London: Chatham House, 1971.

Mayne, Richard. *The Institutions of the European Community*. London: Chatham House, 1968.

Mendras, Henri, and Yves Tavernier, eds. *Terre, paysans, et politique*. Paris: SEDEIS, 1969.

Meynaud, Jean and Dusan Sidjanski. *Les Groupes de pression dans la communauté européenne; 1958-1968*. Brussels: Institut d'Etudes Européennes, 1971.

———. *Science politique et intégration européenne*. Geneva: Institut d'Etudes Européennes, 1965.

Moore, Barrington. *The Social Origins of Dictatorship and Democracy*. Boston: Beacon Press, 1966.

Morgan, Roger. *West European Politics Since 1945: The Shaping of the European Community*. London: Batsford, 1972.

Muth, Hanns Peter. *French Agriculture and the Political Integration of Western Europe*. Leiden, Netherlands: A. W. Sijthoff, 1970.

Nême, Jacques, and Colette Nême. *Economie européenne*. Paris: Presses Universitaires de France, 1970.

Nobis, Friederich. *Das Bundesministerium für Ernährung, Landwirtschaft, und Forsten*. Frankfurt am Main and Bonn: Athenäum Verlag, 1966.

Noelle, Elisabeth, and Erich Peter Neumann. *Jahrbuch der öffentlichen Meinung 1968-1973*. Allensbach and Bonn: Verlag für Demoskopie, 1974.

Organization for Economic Cooperation and Development. *Agricultural Policy in France*. Paris: The Organization, 1974.

———. *Agricultural Policy in Germany*. Paris: The Organization, 1974.

———. *Agricultural Policy of the European Economic Community*. Paris: The Organization, 1973.

———. *Structural Reform Measures in Agriculture*. Paris: The Organization, 1972.

Palmer, Michael, John Lambert et al. *European Unity: A Survey of the European Organizations*. London: Chatham House, 1963.

Pappi, Ugo, and Charles Nunn, eds. *Economic Problems of Agriculture in Industrial Societies*. London: Macmillan, 1969.

Pautard, J. *Les Disparités regionales dans la croissance de l'agriculture française*. Paris: Gauthier-Villars, 1965.

Puvogel, Curt. *Der Weg Zum Landwirtschaftsgesetz*. Munich: Bayerischer Landwirtschaftsverlag, 1957.

Quaden, Guy. *Parité pour l'agriculture et disparité entre agriculteurs*. The Hague, Netherlands: Martinus Nijhoff, 1973.

Reboul, Lawrence, and Albert Te Pass, eds. *La Lettre Mansholt: Réactions et Commentaires*. Paris: J. J. Pauvert, 1972.

Rosenthal, Glenda Goldstone. *The Men Behind the Decisions: Cases in European Policy-Making*. Lexington, Mass.: Lexington Books, 1975.

Roussillon, Henry. *L'Association Générale des Producteurs de Blé*. Paris: Fondation Nationale des Sciences Politiques, 1970.

Schlotter, H. G., ed. *Die Willensbildung in der Agrarpolitik*. Munich: BLV Verlagsgesellschaft, 1971.

Stein, Eric, and Peter Hay, eds. *Documents for Use with Cases and Materials on the Law and Institutions of the Atlantic Area*. Ann Arbor, Mich.: The Overbeck Company, 1963.

Stolper, Gustav. *The German Economy: 1870 to the Present*. New York: Harcourt, Brace & World, 1967.

Suleiman, Ezra. *Politics, Power, and Bureaucracy in France*. Princeton, N.J.: Princeton University Press, 1974.

Symposium Europa: 1950-1970. Bruges, Belgium: College of Europe, 1971.

Tavernier, Yves. *Le Syndicalisme paysan: FNSEA, CNJA*. Paris: Fondation Nationale des Sciences Politiques, 1969.

Tavernier, Yves, Michel Gervais, and Claude Servolin, eds. *L'Univers politique des paysans*. Paris: Armand Colin, 1972.

Tracy, Michael. *Agriculture in Western Europe*. London: Jonathan Cape, 1964.

Virieu, François-Henri de. *La Fin d'une agriculture*. Paris: Calmann-Levy, 1967.

Wallace, Helen. *National Governments and the European Communities*. London: Chatham House, PEP, 1973.

Warnecke, Steven Joshua, ed. *The European Community in the 1970's.* New York: Praeger, 1972.

Watson, Alan. *Europe at Risk.* London: George G. Harrap, 1972.

Wer ist Wer? Frankfurt am Main: Societäts-Verlag, 1973.

Williams, Philip M., and Martin Harrison. *Politics and Society in de Gaulle's Republic.* New York: Anchor, 1971.

Willis, F. Roy. *France, Germany, and the New Europe.* London: Oxford University Press, 1968.

Wright, Gordon. *Rural Revolution in France.* Stanford, Calif.: Stanford University Press, 1964.

Zeller, Adrien. *L'Imbroglio agricole du Marché Commun.* Paris: Calmann-Levy, 1970.

ARTICLES AND PERIODICALS

Agra-Europe, 1965-75.

Baudin, Pierre. "Crises monétaires et politique agricole commune d'août 1969 à juillet 1973." *Revue du Marché commun* (August-September 1973): 309-18.

Brulé, Michel. "Référendum d'avril et l'élection présidentielle de juin 1969: L'élection présidentielle." *Sondages* (1969): 37-72.

"The Common Agricultural Policy Market Organizations and Price Systems." *Newsletter of the Common Agricultural Policy* 4 (September 1972): 3-12.

Common Market, 1966-70.

Deleau, Jean. Report to the *Assemblée Permanente des Chambres d'Agriculture,* "Compte-rendu, APCA, Session Extraordinaire, 76e, 4-5 septembre 1974." *Chambres d'Agri-culture* 541-42, supplement (October 1-15, 1974): 34-37.

Delorme, Hélène. "Le rôle des forces paysannes dans l'élaboration de la politique agricole commune." *Revue française de science politique* 19 (April 1969): 356-91.

Edinger, Lewis. "Political Change in Germany." *Comparative Politics* 2 (July 1970): 549-78.

"L'Élection présidentielle de décembre 1965: L'élection présidentielle et les sondages pré-électoraux." *Sondages* (1965): 7-38.

"L'Élection présidentielle des 5 et 19 mai 1974." *Sondages* (1974): 7-38.

"Les élections législatives des 4 et 11 mars 1973." *Sondages* (1973): 20-21.

"L'Europe agricole et l'élargissement du Marché Commun." *Notes et Etudes Documentaires* (February 12, 1974): 4061-63.

Feld, Werner J. "Diplomatic Behavior in the European Community: Milieus and Motivations." *Journal of Common Market Studies* 11 (September 1972): 18-25.

——. "National Economic Interest Groups and Policy Formation in the EEC." *Political
Science Quarterly* 80 (1966): 392-411.

Frankfurter Allgemeine Zeitung, 1965-75.

Hallett, G. "Agricultural Policy in West Germany." *Journal of Agricultural Economy* 19
(January 1968): 87-95.

Heidhues, Theodor. "Voraussetzungen und Möglichkeiten einer Neuorientierung in der
Agrarpolitik." *Agrarwirtschaft* 33 (1969): 5-36.

Herald Tribune, 1974-75.

Klingemann, Hans D. and Franz Urban Pappi. "Les élections legislatives des 23 et 30 juin
1968." *Sondages* (1968): 97-116.

——. "The 1969 Bundestag Election in the Federal Republic of Germany." *Comparative
Politics* 2 (July 1970): 519-33.

Labrousse, Jeanne. "Les Sondages et les élections de mars 1967." *Sondages* (1967): 11-64.

Le Monde, 1965-75.

McLin, Jon. "Europe's Common Agricultural Policy in a Time of Shortages." *American
Universities Field Staff Reports*, West European Series, 8 (1973).

——. "Western Europe and the World Food Problem." *American Universities Field Staff
Reports*, West European Series, 9 (1975).

Neunreither, Karlheinz. "Transformation of a Political Role: Reconsidering the Case of the
Commission of the European Communities." *Journal of Common Market Studies* 10
(1972): 233-48.

Nielsen, Terkel T. "Aspects of the EEC Influence of European Groups in the Decision-
Making Process: The Common Agricultural Policy." *Government and Opposition* 6
(Autumn 1971): 539-58.

Pickles, William. "Political Power in the EEC." *Journal of Common Market Studies* 2
(1963): 63-84.

Le Producteur Agricole Français, 1973-75.

"Le Royaume Uni et la CEE: Comment trouver des éléments d'entente?" *Paysans* (April-
May 1974), special issue.

Schneider, H. "Les groupes de pression." *Documents* (Cologne) 21 (September-October
1966): 43-55.

Tavernier, Yves. "Le M.O.D.E.F.," *Revue française de science politique* 18 (June 1968): 542-63.

——. "Les paysans et la politique." *Revue française de science politique* 12 (September 1962): 599-646.

——. "Le syndicalisme paysan et la Cinquième République, 1962-1965." *Revue française de science politique* 16 (October 1966): 869-912.

"Eine vermeidbare Spaltung." *Deutsche Landwirtschaftliche Presse*, August 8, 1972.

PUBLIC DOCUMENTS

Commission of the European Communities. *The Agricultural Situation in the Community*. Brussels: November, 1974.

——. *General Report on the Activities of the European Communities*. Brussels: annual.

Economic Development Committee for Agriculture. *U.K. Farming and the Common Market: Milk and Milk Products*. London: National Economic Development Office, 1973.

Federal Republic of Germany, Deutscher Bundestag. *Agrarbericht 1972 der Bundesregierung, Materialband*. Bonn: 1972.

——. *Bericht der Bundesregierung über die Lage der Landwirtschaft gemäss 4 Landwirtschaftsgesetz und Massnahmen der Bundesregierung gemäss 5 Landwirtschaftsgesetz und EWG-Anpassungsgesetz*. Bonn: 1970.

Federal Republic of Germany, Press and Information Office of the Federal Government. *The German Federal Government*. Bonn: 1969.

Home-Grown Cereals Authority. *Background to the EEC Cereal Market*. London: Home-Grown Cereals Authority, 1972.

UNPUBLISHED MATERIALS

Braun, Gerald. "Die Rolle der Wirtschaftsverbände in agrarpolitischen Entscheidungsprozess der Europäi-schen Wirtschaftsgemeinschaft." Unpublished Ph.D. dissertation, Economics Department, Albert Ludwigs Universität, 1971.

Comité des Organisations Professionnelles Agricoles, Assembly. Documents and Resolutions.

——, General Experts. Documents.

——, Presidium. Minutes.

——. Press releases.

Delorme, Hélène. Etude de la Représentation des Agriculteurs dans la C.E.E., Rapport provisoire sur l'enguête effectuée en vertu de la Convention no. 18 du 10 mai 1971 entre le Cordes et la F.N.S.P." Paris: Fondation Nationale des Sciences Politiques, Centre d'Etudes des Relations Internationales, n.d.

Deutscher Bauernverband der Landwirte im Nebenberuf. Documents.

Keeler, John. "The Political and Structural Impact of the EEC on National Interest Groups: The Case of French Agricultural Syndicalism." Unpublished paper, 1975.

Mathy, Chantal. "Essai d'analyse politique du Comité des Organisations Professionnelles Agricoles de la CEE." Unpublished memoir, Louvain, Belgium, 1968.

INTERVIEW SOURCES

Association Générale des Producteurs de Blé. Paris.

Comité des Organisations Professionnelles Agricoles. Brussels.

Commission of the European Communities. Brussels.

Deutscher Bauernverband. Bonn.

Economic and Social Council of the European Communities. Brussels.

Federal Republic of Germany. Ministry of Food, Agriculture, and Forests. Brussels.

Fédération Nationale des Syndicats d'Exploitants Agricoles. Paris.

France. Ministry of Agriculture.

Permanent Representatives of the Federal Republic of Germany to the European Communities. Brussels.

Permanent Representatives of the French Republic to the European Communities. Brussels.

INDEX

Adenauer, Konrad, 2, 10, 45
Association Générale des Producteurs de
Blé (General Association of Wheat Pro-
ducers, AGPB), 29, 35, 48-58, 71;
adaptation of to Fifth Republic, 48-49,
56; and grain Eurogroup, 86-87; and
Mansholt, 54-56
Aussiedlung program, 15

Baden-Württemburg, 14
Bavaria, 13, 14, 64, 104-05
beef (see, common agricultural policy:
livestock, France, Germany)
Belgium, 64, 106, farmers' organizations
in, 89; national aid to agriculture in,
110
Bonnet, Christian, 81, 105-06
border taxes (see, monetary compensation
amounts)
Brandt, Willy, 18, 111
Brittany, 24, 28, 31, 59, 66

Centre National des Jeunes Agriculteurs
(National Center of Young Farmers,
CNJA), 4, 40; as legitimate farm
spokesman, 14, 27, 30, 34, 39, 103;
and Mansholt Plan, 111; and Ministry
of Agriculture, 34; and structural
policy, 48, 50-51
Centre National Interprofessionnel de
l'Economie Laitière (National Interpro-
fessional Center for Dairy Produce,
CNIEL), 31, 37
Chaban Delmas, Jacques, 32, 33
Chambres d'Agriculture (Chambers of
Agriculture), 24, 30, 35
Chirac, Jacques, 31-33, 36-37, 59, 109-10
Christian Democratic Union (CDU): coali-
tion with Free Democrats, 46, 63;
coalition with Socialists, 10, 64-65;
and farmers, 2, 9-11, 19, 23
Cointat, Michel, 81
Comité de Gueret (Gueret Committee),
24, 34

Comité des Organisations Professionnelles
Agricoles (Committee of Professional
Farm Organizations, COPA): budget
of, 76-78; and Commission, 79, 90-91;
and Committee of Permanent Representatives, 81-82; and Council, 80-81;
and EC decision-making process, 101-
06; and EC grain market, 47; and Economic and Monetary Union, 96; institutions of, 75-76, 78-79; leadership of,
75; and Mansholt Plan, 55-56; membership in, 73-74; and monetary compensation amounts, 95-96; and price policy, 91-96; staff of, 78; and structural
policy, 91-95; as supranational interest
group, 2, 39, 71-72, 115-16; weaknesses of, 82-90
Comité Européen pour le Progrès Agricole
(European Committee for Agricultural
Progress, COMEPRA), 87-88, 115
Commission: a common agricultural policy, 47, 54-56, 67; and COPA, 79, 82-
88; in decision-making process, 1, 3-
4, 58; nationalization of, 83-86
Committee of Permanent Representatives
(CPR), 72, 81-82
common agricultural policy (CAP): and
annual price review, 78; and EC
farmers, 1-2, 31; and French farmers,
31; general framework of, 4-5; and
German farmers, 7, 14-15; and grain,
36-37, 43-58; and livestock, 36-38, 59-
67; 108-10; and Mansholt Plan, 16-17;
and market intervention, 31, 35-36,
50-53, 57; and milk, 36, 60-67; and
price policy, 9, 12-13, 27-29, 31, 36-
38; and structural policy, 16-17, 27-29,
55-56
Confédération Interprofessionnel des Betteraviers Européens (Interprofessional
Confederation of European Sugar Beet
Producers, CIBE), 87
Confédération Nationale de l'Elevage (National Livestock Confederation, CNE),
29

ABOUT THE AUTHOR

WILLIAM F. AVERYT, JR. is Assistant Professor of Political Science at the University of South Alabama, Mobile. Until 1976, he was a part-time instructor and graduate student at Yale University.

Dr. Averyt has published articles on European politics and the European Community in the *Naval War College Review* and *International Organization*.

Dr. Averyt holds a B.A. degree from the University of Alabama; a *diplôme* from the Centre Universitaire des Hautes Etudes Européennes of the University of Strasbourg, France; an M.A. degree from the Johns Hopkins School of Advanced International Studies, Washington, D.C., and M.Phil. and Ph.D. degrees from Yale University.

THE CONSTRUCTION OF A EUROPEAN COMMUNITY
Achievements and Prospects for the Future
Pierre Maillet

EUROPEAN ECONOMIC ISSUES
Agriculture, Economic Security, Industrial Democracy,
the OECD
Atlantic Studies—III

THE FINANCES OF EUROPE
Daniel Strasser

ASSOCIATION SYSTEM OF THE EUROPEAN COMMUNITY
Jacqueline D. Matthews

DECISION MAKING IN THE EUROPEAN COMMUNITY
Christoph Sasse
Edward Poullet
David Coombes
Gérard Deprez